Catholic Women and Abortion

Stories of Healing

Edited by
Pat King

Sheed & Ward

Anchor symbol description is from *Our Sunday Visitor's Catholic Dictionary*, ed. by Rev. Peter M.J. Stravinskas, ©1993 by Our Sunday Visitor, Inc. Reprinted by permission.

Sheed & Ward™ is a service of The National Catholic Reporter Publishing Company.

Library of Congress Cataloguing-in-Publication Data

Catholic women and abortion : stories of healing / edited by Pat King.
     p.   cm.
  ISBN: 1-55612-715-4 (acid free)
   1. Abortion—Religious aspects—Catholic Church. 2. Women, Catholic—Psychology. I. King, Pat 1934-.
HQ767.3.C38 1994
241'.6976—dc20   94-14612
                                              CIP

Published by: Sheed & Ward
               115 E. Armour Blvd.
               P.O. Box 419492
               Kansas City, MO 64141

To order, call: (800) 333-7373

Contents

The anchor is an ancient symbol of hope, courage, safety, and confidence, as in the N.T.: "Hold fast the hope set before us which we have as the anchor for the soul" (Heb 6:19). It was used as a symbol for the cross of Christ, to be kept secret among the Christians and unrecognizable by the unbelievers. It appears on early Christian sarcophagi as a symbol of the hope in the resurrection.

Foreword

"A sound is heard in Ramah, the sound of bitter weeping. Rachel mourns her children, she refuses to be consoled because her children are no more. Thus says the Lord: Cease your cries of mourning. Wipe the tears from your eyes. The sorrow you have shown shall have its reward. There is hope for your future."

—Jeremiah 31:15-17

The sound of women's voices crying out throughout the land, weeping for their lost children, speaking the truth of their abortion experiences, telling of the pain and suffering they have endured—these voices are calling out to be heard. Their cries are being etched into the collective consciousness of a nation. The pain is overwhelming but the good news is that there is hope for the future. The Rachels of today who cry out for their lost children are being heard, and they are being called to healing, just as the Rachel of Scripture was.

In this book Pat King has gathered for the first time the stories of Catholic women who are willing to share with others their experiences of loss, pain and healing. Other books have been written where women share their pain, but, ironically, none of them have dealt with the journeys of Catholic women.

In 1975 the Catholic bishops of the United States issued a document calling for an outreach of reconciliation and healing for those whose lives have been changed irrevocably by an abortion. This was truly a prophetic call, for no one in this country knew the full effect of abortion's aftermath, much less what was involved in its healing. In 1984 Project Rachel was founded to reach out to those within the Church who were struggling. Yet it is only now, more than 10 years later, that some of these stories are being shared more widely.

It is my hope that all who read this book will be touched by the pain and the courage of these women who undertook their healing journeys. I pray that what clearly shines through these stories is the patient and persistent love of our God who pursues us relentlessly with truly unconditional love, infinite mercy and tender care. May this book encourage those who are hurting to begin their healing journey. May it challenge those who know someone who is hurting to reach out to them in love. And may it lead everyone who reads it to a deeper, more compassionate understanding of the wound that occurs when a child is lost through an abortion and to a deeper personal encounter with their God, recognizing how God has touched their lives when they least expected it.

If you are touched by what you read here and wish to speak to someone, The National Office of Post-Abortion Reconciliation and Healing will refer you to someone near you who can journey with you. The national referral number is 1-800-5WE-CARE.

Vicki Thorn, Executive Director
National Office of Post-Abortion
Reconciliation and Healing
September 18, 1993

Preface

In this book are the stories of Patsy, Liane, Marie, Liz, Heidi, and Maureen. All but one, Catholics from infancy. Raised in a moral atmosphere, although differing in degrees, each woman knew that abortion was wrong. Each knew, at some level, that if she had an abortion she was separating herself from God. But in the depth of her crisis, each chose an abortion.

What happened emotionally and spiritually as a result? When a woman chooses an abortion and goes against her own moral code, she experiences such psychological distress that she must look for any way that will reduce it.[1]

She does this by denial:

---

1. Festinger, L. (1957) A theory of cognitive dissonance, Stanford, CA: Stanford University Press.

"I didn't know it was a baby."

"I didn't know it was wrong."

"I don't believe I've hurt anyone."

Or she persuades herself that what she's done was for others:

"I did it for the good of my other children."

"I did it for my parents, my pregnancy would kill them."

"I did it for the good of the child, there was no money to care for it."

The greater the discrepancy between belief and behavior, the stronger the inner distress becomes, until a woman who has chosen an abortion against her own belief system must, for her own survival, stay locked into her new pattern of belief. Yet, morally she remains at odds with it. This causes her to act in strange and often compulsive ways.

This is the dilemma of the women whose stories are told in this book. All the stories are different, yet all have the same underlying theme:

I cannot face what I have done, yet I live in devastating inner conflict when I don't face it.

Each woman takes us on a deeply personal journey of her abortion distress: from the choice that set the process in motion, into the valley of denial, through the complicated conflicts that follow, to the healing at journey's end.

These women are not alone. 400,000 Catholic women a year are having abortions. Each one who believes that abortion is wrong will need to deny the gravity of her choice. As time goes by and the inner conflict becomes too painful to bear, each must search for a solution to that pain.

If you are one of these women, or if you are her husband or a member of her family, and you are beginning to make even a small attempt to look at those places in your history that forever changed a life, this is your book. These women's stories are connected to yours. In showing you their pathways to healing, they can point you to your own.

1

Hiding from Myself

Patsy Fields

t

I still can't understand how I got hooked up with Les. He was into liberal arts and I was into sciences. He was 5'6" and I was 5'10". He loved sports and I, at the time, thought they were a waste of time.

Yet we fell deeply in love. I was a virgin and Les never pushed me on the issue of sex. But as our love grew, I knew that I wanted to share something very precious with him. After three months we made love. He always used a condom and we never seriously considered the possibility of pregnancy. However, I thought it would be a good idea to get on the pill. A gynecologist examined me and asked, "Is your period late this month?"

"Yes, but only a couple of days."

"Have your breasts been hurting?"

"As a matter of fact, they were really bothering me a week or so ago, but I didn't think anything about it."

The doctor nodded, "Well, you're already pregnant and so you obviously don't need the pill at this point. You're not married are you?"

I shook my head no. Strangely, I had no reaction to being told I was pregnant. It wasn't an option I had ever considered.

When I told him I wasn't married, he replied, "Well, don't worry. Abortion is legal now."

"Then that's what I'll do." I never stopped to think about what I was doing, I certainly never prayed about it. I blindly accepted this man's offer of an abortion and absolutely denied that this might be a baby. I went out to the waiting room and told Les the news, "The doctor says I'm pregnant, but he'll make arrangements for an abortion." End of conversation. We told no one, not even my sister who lived with me.

The abortion was scheduled for Friday, but the day before I just happened to run into a priest at the Student Union Building. I pulled him out into the hall, "Father, I had this abortion that I need to confess." At the time I thought it was pretty clever to confess a sin before I even committed it.

The priest listened to my story and said, "You are forgiven for what you've done. You must now try to put this behind you and go on with your life." I naively thought I had taken charge of one more obstacle in my life.

Taking charge was something I was good at. I'd been doing it for as long as I could remember . . .

I'm the oldest of five children and my mother never seemed to have a lot of time or patience with me, so I had to manage things for myself. Yet the fact that I could take charge of any situation I was in, and didn't demand a lot of her attention, made me feel that she helped the other children more.

But I would have loved more of Mom's time. I remember how I laid in bed and tried to figure a way I could get her to love me more. I thought maybe if I slept with my arms next to my body like the baby held hers, it would remind Mom of when I was a baby. I went to sleep every night trying to be in that position. But I don't think it ever made any difference to her.

So I decided to be as perfect as I could be and not bother her. That way it felt like it was my choice not to have any of her time.

One day I came home in tears because a friend had hurt my feelings. My mother caught me off guard by asking, "Is there anything the matter, or are you just having an off day?"

I felt shocked that she cared enough to ask. But I had decided to be perfect and no bother and so I answered her, "I'm not having any trouble at all."

This became the pattern of my growing up years: deny any problems; take charge; appear perfect and people will like you.

My best physical traits were my long blond hair and blue eyes. As the years went on I grew to be tall and slender. College presented no challenges because academics were easy. I usually had dates when I wanted them. Spiritually, I was an average Catholic of the early 70s. I went to Mass every Sunday and occasionally darkened the confessional door. But there was no real knowledge of the Lord in my life, no idea where a Bible might be found in our home, no prayer life.

So there I was at 19, taking charge of my life by scheduling an abortion that, deep within me, I must have known was wrong.

Yet I was striving to be perfect. I managed this contradiction by simply not facing the situation.

The next morning I went to a little out-of-the-way medical facility. Strapped to a table, I counted backwards to 97 before forgetting everything else. The next thing I knew, I was in a hospital bed and a nurse was checking me. Groggily I asked her, "When will I start my next period?"

"Now don't be worried. Everything is going to be okay."

A couple of hours later I went home. I had no pain or regret or even relief. I was still in total denial that this might have been a baby.

Wondering when my next period would start turned out to be an ominous concern. Several weeks went by. My period did not begin and my tummy started to grow. Les and I had decided not to have sex again until everything was back to normal, so I knew I hadn't conceived again. I went to another lab for another test.

Pregnant. I was floored. I reached for the phone and called the first doctor's nurse. "This is Patsy Murphy. I had an abortion but I'm still pregnant."

"Miss Murphy, I think you'd better come in right away."

I had planned on never seeing that doctor again but there I was being examined by him. He shook his head, "You're definitely still pregnant. But I know that we got out fetal tissue before so you must have part of a baby growing inside of you." He stopped and thought, "You're too far along to do another D&C, so what I'd like to do is wait a little while until you are larger and then we'll do a saline injection."

"*Part of a baby.*" How those words haunted me. I wondered what parts were still left. Les stuck with me through all of this, but we both knew it was just a matter of time before our relationship ended. It couldn't stand the stress of this ongoing "medical problem."

By now I was four months pregnant and I think my sister suspected something. "Patsy, your stomach sure is growing."

I laughed, "You're right. I need to go on a diet."

Because my hair was falling out in droves she added, "I've heard that sometimes when you're pregnant your hair falls out."

Once again I refused to admit I had a problem. I laughed, "It's because of my dandruff."

Also concerned was a good friend, Mike, who later became a priest. We were sitting outside the cathedral one morning and he asked, "Patsy, you seem so sick. Is there anything I can help you with?"

Typically, I took charge, once more making sure I was no bother. "Oh Mike, you're such a worrier. Of course I'm fine. I just need to get through finals."

After finals I returned to the out-of-the-way facility. The doctor injected my uterus with saline, "Be sure and let me know if this hurts."

"It's bound to hurt having that big needle placed in my belly."

"I mean if it really hurts, because that may mean I've injected the wrong area."

I cringed at the thought.

The saline should have induced labor within 24 to 48 hours but absolutely nothing happened. The doctor reinjected my uterus. "Whatever is in there is definitely dead now, so we'll just have to wait."

Wait I did. Four days of limbo, sitting around, denying the gravity of my situation. Finally I went into labor and delivered that "part of a baby."

Two days later, alone in the apartment, my breasts filled with milk. Milk. Nourishment for a baby I'd denied existed. I sat on the edge of the bed, feeling sick and numb.

A baby. What had I done? The tears fell at last. I somehow managed to find the priest that I had first confessed my abortion to. I sobbed as I told him the truth about the first confession and what had since happened.

The priest didn't scold but repeated the counsel he'd given before, "Go on with your life now, you've been forgiven."

The real grace was that I knew the Lord had forgiven me. I never questioned it for a moment. Just as I had accepted the doctor's simple offer of an abortion, I also freely accepted the Lord's forgiveness through this priest.

Life went on, but it was never to be the same.

* * *

I finished college and began working in the lab of a local hospital. This is where I met Andy Fields, a tall, dark, rather studious young intern. He was also a practicing Catholic and we had much in common besides just having a good time together. After three months of dating we truly fell in love and Andy proposed.

We had been married two years when I met him at the door with good news. "Guess what, hon, I'm pregnant." He was delighted. But ten weeks later I started spotting and cramping. I slumped into a chair, terrified I was miscarrying. Only I knew why. God was punishing me.

Sometime after the miscarriage I told my mother, "I would have named the child Lisa if it had been a girl."

"That's a nice name, would you use it again?"

"No, Mom, that was for the other baby." I sensed that "the other baby" I was talking about was the aborted one and I couldn't replace her by giving her name away. But I turned such thoughts away. The abortion was a deep, painful undercurrent that I was not ready to have surface.

I conceived again. This pregnancy proceeded smoothly until about six months when I began bleeding and was diagnosed with placenta previa. I was sure God would punish me with another miscarriage. But by now I'd felt the baby move and kick and I knew how completely formed it was. I pleaded with God, "Please let the baby live." I focused all my energy and prayer on the baby and wouldn't let the abortion enter my mind.

Through conservative medical treatment and over nine weeks in the hospital, I carried the baby to term and delivered by C-section a large, healthy son. We named him Patrick.

To my great surprise, 13 months later I found myself pregnant again. This was my easiest pregnancy but mentally I was in turmoil. This was an unplanned pregnancy, like the one that was aborted. Anguish began surfacing in me that I couldn't understand. I tried to look back in my past for the reason, but I couldn't seem to reach it.

All I knew was that I didn't like myself and I didn't know why. I felt like I was the most unattractive person around.

When Linda was born I didn't like her either. Bonding with her was difficult, almost impossible. Also, I was in a state of postpartum depression. One day as I took care of the baby, hardly without looking at her, I thought, I must need professional help. I don't understand this depression and confusion at all. Tears rolled down my cheeks.

But I hid all this inner crisis from Andy. I couldn't tell him. I was the "perfect person." I'd always managed everything well. A person like that shouldn't need psychological help. I continued to make a home for Andy and Patrick and Linda, but I lived silently with the turmoil that something was terribly wrong.

* * *

Up to this point I was a "good" Catholic. I attended Mass almost every weekend and knew I'd missed something if I couldn't make it to the service. However, I wasn't involved in the church and I felt no real sense of community with the parish. Fortunately, there were lots of mature Catholics around, many of whom were patients of Andy's, who kept after us to become more active.

One thing I kept hearing about was Parish Renewal. This entailed giving up a Friday evening, Saturday and Sunday, and, believe me, I had absolutely no desire to sacrifice so much for anyone. I thought that calling that much time at church a "renewal" was a misnomer for certain. However, every time one was scheduled, dozens of people urged me to attend. Finally I told Andy, "I'm going just to get these fanatics off my back. Don't worry, I won't spend all day Saturday and Sunday at church because I'll be too exhausted to participate."

The Lord tolerated my kicking and screaming because he knew he had a conversion in store for me. The renewal awak-

ened in my heart the real joy of being a
Catholic.   I discovered the importance of
community, scripture, prayer and being a
Catholic Christian. As for those killer hours
that I swore I'd never keep, I came home at
11:00 each evening so fired up that I
wanted to wake up Andy and tell him everything.

Besides spiritual renewal, another important thing happened that weekend: the
powers that be in the parish saw a side of
me they hadn't seen before. They decided
to help me "develop" my gifts and talents.
My number one spiritual gift is organization
and the parish staff quickly tapped into
that.

Several years of a truly Camelot existence
followed.   I liked myself, loved the Lord,
found ego support in my church work.   I
learned to accept my daughter, even though
we weren't close.   Only occasionally were
there sad moments, times so full of torment
that the only way I could survive was not to
let myself think about their origin. I would
remind myself what the confessor priest had
said: get on with my life.

By now I had many good friends in the
parish and I needed very much to keep my
abortion secret. How could anybody like me

if they knew what an awful, sinful woman I was?

Then one Lent, 13 years after the abortion, I believe the Lord decided it was time for me to face my hidden sorrow. Andy and I were Communion distributors at Mass. In the homily the priest started talking about sin. He began mentioning sin after sin, from little white lies to abortion and murder.

Every time he opened his mouth, I heard another sin that this "good" Catholic had committed. I felt like the woman at the well must have felt when Jesus laid out her sins before her. I wanted to leave that Mass, just get out of there because the litany of my sins was overwhelming.

"God, make him stop," I prayed, but he kept going on and on. I was so distraught I could barely give out Communion, thinking the entire time: *If you only knew what a sinner I am to be giving you the Body of Christ.* I felt like the world's greatest hypocrite.

When Mass was finally over, the pastor and I cleaned up the sacristy and walked to the gym for another function. As we walked cross the dark parking lot I said, "That homily literally devastated me. I am so upset."

He, of course, had no idea of why I was so torn, but simply said, "Well, the good news here, Patsy, is that you can be forgiven for all of this, you know."

Once more I headed for the confessional. By this time my friend from college, Mike, who had been so concerned about me when I was pregnant, was a priest in a little town about one-and-a-half hours from my home. I got up my courage and drove over, and had a long talk and good cry. I confessed and turned away from every sin I'd ever committed. I didn't want to miss one and have it appear in front of me in another homily.

There was so much peace from the act of verbally confessing such serious sin and finding love and forgiveness, that this time I really believed my suffering was over.

But in a couple of weeks the heartache over my abortion was back. Through journaling, I found that I could not even say the word "abortion." My anguish hadn't ended. I realized I had some significant work to do in terms of healing. I went back to see Mike. I had to show him my journal because I was incapable of even verbalizing with him my discomfort with the word.

Then the tears fell and fell and fell. My whole body seemed filled with pain. "Mike, what I did was so terrible I can't face it. Will you help me find healing?"

"Patsy, I wish more than anything I could help you, but I simply can't. I don't know how to help you with this problem."

My heart seemed to break with his words. It's not that I wanted him to give me all of the answers; I wanted the one person I had shared my secret with to be the one to help me find closure for the wound.

Dear God, only you can help me.

Shortly after, at a meeting at the parish, I asked about a Scripture reading with the theme of healing. The associate pastor took me aside and said a totally surprising thing to me. "This scripture is talking about spiritual healing, but many of us have need of psychological healing in our lives also. I've known for some years that you have something in your past that you need help with in resolving."

It was amazing that he picked this particular time to speak of it. I guess that if he had tried to tell me any sooner I would not have listened to him. Prior to this point I had not acknowledged any need for healing. Now I was willing to listen to him and he was able to recommend a psychologist. I said I would call for an appointment.

But when it came right down to it, I couldn't make the appointment. It was just too big a step. I knew a psychologist would make me look at areas of my past that I did not want to examine. I knew that it meant I would have to say the word "abortion." I knew I would have to say aloud that I had killed a child. How could I, I who was still trying to be a perfect person, say words like that? There was almost a war inside of me. "Call the psychologist." "Not today." "Yes." "No." "Do it now." "I can't."

In the middle of this inner dialogue I walked into the living room where my daughter was watching *The Wizard of Oz*. It was at the part where Dorothy and the scarecrow are trying to talk the cowardly lion into coming with them to Oz and he is filled with excuses. Finally they say, "Well, what have you got to lose? You won't be any worse off than you are now."

Those words went straight to my heart. *What have I got to lose?* I went right to the phone and made the call. I couldn't be any worse off than I was right at that moment.

I met with the doctor two days later and told him about the abortion and how I needed help in healing from it. We talked for an hour, and he gave me a homework assignment: to write about the time of the abortion. I absolutely dreaded doing this. All the years since the abortion I'd thought that I could solve the abortion issue by never going back and looking at it. The idea of examining my state of mind was nightmarish. I was totally afraid of saying I'd had an abortion. The thought of facing this introspection was so painful that I just could not do it.

The next morning I woke up encased in fear. I still couldn't bear to admit what I'd done. But before I could begin, my pastor called about something we were planning. His first question was, "How are you?"

"Oh, okay."

"Okay, that's it. Just okay?"

I wanted to say, no, I'm not okay. I'm doing pretty damn lousy, if you must know. But I just said, "Yeah, that's about it, just okay."

He replied, "Oh, come on, Patsy, it's a beautiful day outside. Why don't you enjoy it?"

Halfheartedly I answered, "I'll try."

After we hung up I looked out the window and saw that indeed it was a warm day, very early in spring. I said to God, "Lord, just for today, I'm not going to worry about that abortion and the work I know I need to

do on it.   I'm just going to enjoy today.
Please take care of it for today and I promise I'll think about it tomorrow."

Once the burden was turned over to the
Lord for the day, I found a sense of peace.
About three hours later, as I was mowing
the lawn, I noticed Patrick inside the house
watching me as I mowed.   I thought about
how when he was younger I had put him in
the swing outside so he could get some
fresh air and watch me mow the lawn.
What I hadn't known at the time was that
he had tremendous allergy problems and I
was putting him in a dangerous situation
with all the dust and grass I was stirring
up.   I thought, what an idiot you were back
then, doing something so dangerous to your
child.

"Wait a minute," I said to myself, "you're
judging   yourself   with   information   that
wasn't available to you at the time you were
putting him outside in his swing."   Then, in
a flash of truth, I knew, *the same was true
when I chose the abortion.*

When I went for that abortion, I was not
the same person that I am now.   I couldn't
judge myself today for what I did then.   I
certainly would not do anything like that
again. *I'd hidden from my past for so long*

that I'd also hidden from the fact that I was changed.

When I began to understand that I was a different person now, I could at last face what I'd done when I was 19. No more would I have to keep the abortion deeply hidden from myself.

With that, I was able to write out my assignment from the psychologist. Because this revelation was so meaningful, I thought I'd finally come to the end of dealing with the pain of the abortion.

It was a beginning.

As I continued to grow and work for the diocese, every so often I heard a little voice inside of me that wished I could help someone on a one-to-one basis. It was such a generic wish I asked myself, "Who would come to you for any personal help? All you do is organize."

One day I thought, "Patsy, maybe you could help some other woman recover from her abortion and aftermath." This was such a shaky thought that I put it out of my mind. Revealing myself would leave me far too vulnerable. I was still very much afraid of letting others know my secret, sinful past. I knew it would jeopardize my work because some people might say that anyone with my past should not be in a position of authority.

The Lord, however, continued to chip away at me with this new call and, finally, I admitted it to a close priest friend. He simply asked, "What does Patsy want to do?" I'm not a "feeling" person and I had to look deeply in my heart to find the answer. But there it was. What I really wanted was to help one woman find healing from the pain of her abortion.

At home I made a deal with the Lord: "Lord, I'll cheerfully minister if you will take care of the details. Just send me someone who needs my help."

I had such peace over this that I decided to attend a national conference in Milwaukee on post-abortion counseling. I told my present pastor where I was going and he said, "Bring lots of Kleenex."

I knew he was wrong. I wouldn't be doing any crying there; I was sure I was healed of my abortion experience.

One morning shortly before the conference, as I was talking with a woman who I'd become close to but who knew nothing of my recent calling, she blurted out, "Patsy, you know I'm not married in the Church so I can't go to confession, but I simply have to confess to someone: I had an abortion years ago. I really need some help resolving it."

There was the woman I'd asked God to send me. I almost fell out of my chair. Later I shared with another woman about the deal I'd made with the Lord and how He'd held me to it. Tears came to her eyes, "Patsy, do you know that 28 years ago I had an abortion and just yesterday I told the very first person I've ever told." She, too, wanted help in getting through her pain.

I could hardly believe it. Hadn't I asked the Lord for just one other person to help? Now I had two. My new ministry had begun.

Then it was time to go to the conference on post-abortion healing. Before I left I stopped by the bishop's house and told him all about what I was doing and how I hoped to start Project Rachel in the diocese. He gave me a small Miraculous Medal that I pinned on my clothes because I didn't have time to buy a chain.

So I was off to the conference thinking I would come back with some clear-cut ideas on how to minister to others. I certainly did not think I had more work to do of my own. But the first night there I talked with a woman who counseled several post-abortion groups. I told her, "I never really thought about what I was doing at the time of the abortion, no idea I was carrying a real baby."

She gave me such an astonished look, "Really?"

"Have you ever come across anyone like that?"

"No."

This was such a shock to me and it put me into such a tailspin that I spent most of the first day of the conference crying. I cried partly because there was still another healing to go through and I didn't relish the thought of any more pain. I cried partly because I was disappointed in myself for not realizing that I wasn't as healed as I thought I was. It was just one more example of how striving to be perfect adds pain to every circumstance.

I walked to the Catholic church a few blocks away, taking a big box of Kleenex and I didn't care who saw me. I let the Lord know how furious I felt. "You lured me to Milwaukee supposedly to learn how to help others when all you really wanted me to do was acknowledge those areas of unresolved hurt in my own abortion experience. Lord, it was a cheap trick sending me those two women who I thought needed my help just so I could think I had some calling in this new ministry."

During that hour I came to doubt everything I had ever held sacred, with the exception of the Lord's love and forgiveness. I doubted my call to any healing and any ministry. "And, Lord, I'm never going to minister for you again."

However, in addition to my fury, I begged the Lord, over and over, "Please, show me the areas in my journey that still need healing. I am completely lost here and don't want to stay in this much pain." I was in such anguish. "Please, Lord, help me out of this and bring me some peace. Open my eyes and show me what is left to be done."

The word GRIEVE came to me. Prior to that day I'd said I'd never lost anyone close to me, but now I knew I had in fact lost someone very close to me, my precious daughter, Lisa. While I had cried a billion tears over my abortion, I'd never cried tears of grief over my loss.

At this same time, women who wanted to participate in a memorial service for their lost babies (either through abortion or miscarriage) were asked to sign up for the service. This was the last thing I wanted to do. But I was so close to rock bottom I felt I had nowhere else to go but up.

The service was scheduled for 4:30 the next day. I spent the day in mourning, just like one would for any funeral. I stayed to myself because grieving seemed like such a personal thing, and I really didn't want to just fall apart in front of the other women. (Perfect people don't fall apart!)

When I arrived for the service, I was given a little handkerchief doll with a small pink ribbon. To my surprise, the little handkerchief doll rapidly became real. I found myself wanting to hold her and caress her and put her over my shoulder. I wanted to love her. For those few minutes I bonded with her. As I held and loved my little Lisa, I took off the bishop's medal and pinned it inside of her handkerchief dress—the one gift I could give her. I hoped the bishop wouldn't mind that I gave his gift to my baby.

At one point, as we were seated in that chapel, I started thinking about that "part of a baby" and I thought, I really should rip this doll apart like I did before. But I couldn't do it twice. And then, when it came time to put the babies in the little coffin, to formally give them to the Lord, I almost couldn't part with her. I wanted to hold on just a little longer—I wish even now

I could have held her a little longer. But I had to give her to the Lord.

* * *

For years I've looked forward to seeing her again when we both are in heaven. I know this will happen, but I still miss her now. This, too, is part of grieving.

At last I can say, I'm healed of my abortion. For me, acceptance of God's forgiveness came first and was the easy part. Facing the abortion and realizing that I can't hold myself responsible today for a choice made when I was a different person than I am now was my place of change. Lastly, I found healing in grieving for my lost child and putting closure on her life.

One more thing, now that I am at peace with myself, I am also at peace with my other daughter, Linda.

* * *

Editor's note: Today Patsy Fields has coordinated the Project Rachel program in her diocese.

2

Saturday's Child

by Liane Heron

I was scared at first, yet happy at the thought of a baby growing within me, happy at the thought of being married to this wonderful man. Jim held me tenderly in his arms. "A baby. I'm glad for us, Liane. We'll get married and be a family."

I was nineteen and had been staying with friends. Jim, who was 36, had moved into their basement while he went through his divorce. That was how we met. He treated me like I was special. I, who always felt like a nobody, was for the first time in my life, feeling important. With Jim's love and a baby coming I really was a Somebody.

But as the days went by, Jim seemed less and less enthusiastic about the baby. "Did your period come today?," he asked repeatedly. Tension grew in each asking and an anxiousness welled within me as I realized Jim didn't want the baby after all.

Together we left on a business trip from Seattle to Colorado. On the way I started feeling sick. But Jim was kind and I thought everything was going to be all right. Then just before we started home, we stopped at a bar and met Greg, a friend of Jim's. He took Jim aside and asked if he could spend the night with me.

We got in the car and Jim went crazy, driving like a madman, honking the horn wildly at anything in his way.

"What's eating you?"

He growled, "You know good and well what's eating me."

"No, I don't, what's with you anyway?"

"Greg wants to take you to bed and you can't wait."

I was dumbfounded, "That's not true. Greg's your friend."

Jim drove furiously without a word and pulled up in front of Greg's house. He stopped the car, doubled up his fist and punched me in the face. "Don't you know I love you?" he shouted. He punched me again. My nose bled and I started crying. He reached across me, opened the passenger door and pushed me out on the ground. "This is where you belong."

He drove off and left me lying there.

I was so scared all I could do was cry. I was two-and-a-half-months' pregnant, without any money and in a deserted part of a strange state. It took three days to find someone to loan me airfare and drive me three hours into Denver so I could get a plane home.

When Jim arrived home from his long drive from Colorado, I was already there. He wrapped his arms around me, "Liane, I'm so sorry. Forgive me. I'm sorry. I'm sorry."

He wanted us to get back together. I was pregnant and I needed him. Also, I believed him. Once more he was so kind to me that I thought everything was going to be okay.

The next day Jim said, "I want you to get an abortion."

I was shocked. "I can't do that. I'm a Catholic. I'm a good Catholic girl and I shouldn't even have sex outside of marriage. I can't have an abortion."

That didn't phase him. "I've thought it through and you need an abortion." He glared at me, "I really mean it."

I pleaded with him. "No, I can't." This was his baby and mine and I wanted it.

Jim insisted so much I was afraid I'd back down. I turned to my best friend. Her advice made things worse. "Do it, Liane, get the abortion. Jim's right. A baby will only louse up your life."

I felt so pressured. I wanted my baby but I wanted to please Jim. I thought for a moment that maybe I could call my mother. But I couldn't. I didn't have "permission" to talk about such matters with her.

"I can't do it, Jim. I can't."

He wouldn't relent.

Against my better judgment, against my faith and morals, I walked with Jim to an abortion clinic. The scarred second-hand chairs in the waiting room are all I can remember. I was the last patient to come out of the anesthesia. Maybe I didn't want to come out of it. I'd aborted my first conceived child.

That night my milk came in. My breasts were so full of pain that I cried. "Jim, I really hurt." He worked on his car without answering.

Different. How else can I explain it? I woke up the next morning and I was different. Something was dead, not just the baby, but a part of me. I was empty with an emptiness I couldn't fathom. Empty. Dead. Different.

Within a couple of weeks Jim was seeing another woman. My heart felt broken. I'd gotten dumped in Colorado, then I had an abortion, and next I was abandoned. How could I have fooled myself into thinking I was a Somebody?

* * *

When I go back to the beginning of my life, it's easy to see why I thought of myself as a Nobody. I don't blame my mother, but I know she was not happy to find she was pregnant with me. Several months before her pregnancy, my sister had been severely burned and was in the hospital, a 300-mile round trip through the desert. She spent long days sitting through critical surgery, never knowing if my sister would live or die. My brother was still little, and then there was me coming along to an already over-burdened family.

After my birth, Mom either brought me along to the hospital while she attended my sister or else left me with someone. No fault of Mom's, but we had no opportunity for bonding. I was so withdrawn I didn't talk until I was four.

As I grew older, Mom just didn't have time to listen to me. Even in little things she didn't listen. I remember begging her, "Please don't make me wear a skirt and blouse after school. I wear a uniform all day, please let me dress like the other kids."

"Liane, why are you so difficult? Just do what I say."

She didn't understand that I was embarrassed to be so out of style. When I was nine, my brother began to sexually abuse me but I couldn't tell her. When I couldn't get her to listen to little things, how could I talk to her about sex or anything important like that?

I longed to run free and be who I really was inside. The person inside, who no one else knew, was sensitive and kind, she loved God and wanted to always obey Him. But no one knew about her. Instead, there were five more children and Mom got leukemia. The needs of the household and the person I was inside seemed to be at odds.

"Mom, I cleaned the kitchen; can I go play?"

"Just change the laundry and fix the baby's bottle."

"I did it. Now can I go play?"

"First take out the trash and sweep the floor."

"Now can I go play?" I wanted to please her but I wanted to play, too.

"Liane, why do I have to go through this with you? For goodness sake, can't you see that I need your help here?"

The worst thing that could have happened to me in high school happened. I was raped. I felt humiliated and angry but I couldn't talk about it. I took a million showers, but the violated feeling stayed with me. Then, I was raped again by a man named John, a family friend who I was babysitting for. He told everyone we'd had consensual sex, and someone told Mom.

"Liane," she confronted me, "how could you? You went to Catholic school. You know better."

I wanted to tell her what really happened. I looked at the floor. I looked at the ceiling. *Mama, he raped me. I didn't do it with him like he said. I was raped before, too. Leroy, your own precious son, did things to me. Mama, help me.* I said nothing.

"Liane, I'm ashamed of you, deeply ashamed."

Shortly after that I moved out. That was when I met Jim.

* * *

After the abortion I thought everything would be okay if I could just get to confession. The priest was a friend of mine and he smiled as he gave me absolution. I felt sick. Why did he smile? He was supposed to beat me up, call me names and tell me he was ashamed. Didn't he know that? I walked away from the Sacrament totally confused. I couldn't possibly be forgiven.

Men. That's what I did. Men in dance halls. Men in bars. Men from work. Single men, married men. When I was with a man I felt less dead, less disassociated from life. Somehow a man kept me from thinking about my dead child.

I had no conscience. After being in bed with someone, I didn't think anything of it. My involvement with a man whose marriage was on the rocks sent his marriage over the edge. It was not a big deal to me.

My actions with men told me what I needed to hear, the words the priest wouldn't say: I was a nothing, no good, worthless. Yet, I never stopped going to Mass or praying daily. A heavy fog had rolled in over my life but somewhere in that fog there was God, and I knew I needed Him in my life.

By now I was 21 and my new interest, Leo, was 31. He was from another country, had never been around women and refused to date any of the women at work. I was challenged to get this guy to ask me out. Finally, he stopped at my work station. "Liane, you did me a favor. Now I do one for you. I will go to the movies with you."

For me, sex was routine. Later I found out that to Leo it meant everything. Feelings between us ran strong. Most important, he was someone I could play with. We had such fun together; hiking, camping and studying nature. But many of our talks left me upset. Leo had strange ideas about women. They were inferior, they were the property of their husbands. Later I discovered that Leo's father beat his wife and that Leo did not think that at all strange.

But for the present he was generous and kind and we moved in together. Once again I discovered I was pregnant. I stood at the window of our apartment and tried to assess my feelings. The thrill of that first pregnancy didn't exist this time. Leo wanted an abortion but to me it was unthinkable.

He grew adamant, "You must have an abortion."

"No, I'm carrying your child."

"Not a child, a blob of tissue."

"I won't do it."

"Why are you so difficult? I am the man. I decide." The kind, generous Leo was gone. He was absolute authority. "I say abortion. My family will be disgraced."

I could not fight him. Instead I turned to my doctor. He heard my story and told me an abortion was the only answer. The appointment was made from his office.

At home I told Leo, "The abortion is scheduled." Then he was kind again. I responded to his kindness and began to tell myself that doing the abortion would be okay because it pleased Leo and made his life a lot easier.

I have almost no memory of the abortion. It was like sex. I felt numb towards it and just wanted to get it over with. I left the clinic with the ache in my heart that I had killed my second conceived child.

From then on I hated Leo. If he touched me, my stomach ached and I got creepy feelings all over. We stayed together for a year but in separate bedrooms.

After the abortion I was deeply sorrowful. Once more I had to get to confession. Ashamed, I put the abortion in the middle of my other sins. The priest didn't say one word about it. Once more I left the Sacrament feeling empty and ugly. I desperately needed the priest to help me in some way so that I could feel forgiven.

When at last Leo and I broke up, I felt free. I felt like I could breathe fresh air again. Then, a year later, he called. "I need to talk to you."

"I can't see you."

"Please, I must talk to you. Liane, I think of you all the time. Please."

I gave in. I will always regret it.

We went to a favorite hiking place and shared a day rich in conversation. Before the day was out he asked me to marry him. I said yes. I felt Leo was different and that a dream I'd always had, to be a happy family living close to God, was going to be fulfilled.

Back at home, I changed my mind about marrying Leo. He hadn't changed after all and I knew marriage was a mistake. Yet I seemed to have no power to take control and say, No, I don't want this. And also, I was pregnant.

The parish deacon handling our wedding gave us the choice of counseling or an Engaged Encounter. We chose the Encounter, the worst weekend of my life. Leo and I couldn't dialogue, we couldn't agree, we had no goals in common. Despite any actions that made any sense, we were married in June.

On our wedding night, we went into the jacuzzi in our honeymoon suite. Several times Leo splashed hot water in my face, stinging me. "Stop it," I finally said.

Furious, that I had spoken like that, he got out of the water, got into the king-sized bed, way over on the left side and totally ignored me. I came to bed and lay in the middle, feeling alone and confused, wondering what I should do.

Leo, at last, "fulfilled his obligation" but said nothing. Humiliation poured over me, and fear. Here I'd just married in the Catholic Church. What had I done?

I wonder now if I married Leo because I wanted to be abused. Did I deserve abuse because I was a terrible person?

The next 10 years were never-ending punishment. Each morning I woke up in deep emotional pain, like an eggbeater continually grinding inside of me. I knew my life was all wrong and I tried to come up with solutions. I planned often how I could commit myself to a mental institution. Many times I cut myself seriously when I was cooking. When I drove, I fought myself not to crash the car against the freeway wall. When I ran the garbage disposal, I struggled with myself not to put my hand in it and mutilate myself.

Leo and I had three children whom I took care of but wouldn't put my arms around. If one of them came to me looking for a hug, I pretended to be busy. Did I want the two who were dead instead? I don't know. Did I not like my children because I didn't like myself? I don't know.

Most of the time, we lived in a three-way chasm. Me here, the kids there, and Leo in his own room, separated from us all, not talking to us, not eating with us, not having any fun, not going anywhere with us except to the store.

The only light in the bleakness of my life was my longing for God. Over and over I went to the Sacrament of Reconciliation because I desperately needed to be forgiven enough to receive Holy Communion. But two or three weeks after confessing my abortions, I'd feel dirty all over again. The one thing I needed, the strength of Communion, I denied myself until I could once more get to reconciliation and confess again my sinful secret.

I wanted my children to know about God, but Leo refused to allow prayer in his house. Young Leo asked, "Mama, why do we have to hide from Daddy when we pray?"

"We have to." That's all I could say. It wasn't safe to go against Leo. My long-ago dream of a happy family had disappeared into the fog. *Oh God, help me, help me, help me.*

* * *

Help came in an extraordinary way. It was during the first week of Lent. After the children were asleep, I knocked on Leo's door. "Can I come in?" I sat on the edge of his bed and whispered my news. "I'm pregnant."

Leo pounded on his desk. "No more children. I cannot save enough money for anymore children. This is too much. You will have an abortion."

"No."

"Get an abortion or I will divorce you. You will not have one penny. You will not even have a house. You will have nothing."

"No abortion."

"You think this over because I mean what I say. You will be out on the sidewalk."

"Leo . . ."

He turned his back and shut me out.

I went to my room in tears. I know that part of me wanted to be free of him, but another part of me felt sick that he would throw me away because I was pregnant.

Each day Leo pressured me to get the abortion. Before, I had turned to a friend and a doctor. This time I turned to God. I knelt beside my bed, "Oh, dear God, I know I'm a sinner but I need you. Help me to be obedient. Help me not to destroy my child."

I grew stronger in my resolve and stronger in my faith.

Leo raged and God reminded me that Jesus said those who are persecuted for the sake of righteousness are blessed. Leo threatened and God reminded me that He would never leave me or forsake me. Often I talked to the Blessed Mother. Faith grew and I held firm. My child was not going to be aborted. The pleaser inside of me was beginning to lose power.

On Good Friday Leo changed his mind. "I will not divorce you, but from now on you will pay for anything you use. I will not pay one thing for you." Even with that stipulation I was greatly relieved.

In my sixth month, the baby died and naturally aborted. I laid in the hospital bed perfectly at peace because I knew that this time I'd done what God wanted: I'd protected life. I looked up at the ceiling and begged God again for help for my children and myself.

Soon after that God gave me a gift: a kind and godly priest named Father Joseph. Every week he made time in his schedule just to listen to me. It was the most wonderful experience I'd ever had. Also, he prayed with me. I told him my whole story (except, of course, for the abortions which I kept hidden at all times, except for the secrecy of the confessional.)

Never was a friendship so rewarding to me as his. It meant the world to have one person who cared about the sorrow in my life. But I grew uneasy about the deception of not mentioning the abortions. "You need to tell him," I told myself.

But if I did I knew he would hate me and I couldn't take that chance. A little voice inside of me counseled, "You won't be healed until you're honest."

"How can I tell anyone?"

"You must tell the truth."

At a picnic table in a remote campground, I wrote the letter that uncovered my sin. As I wrote, I began to cry. With each word I cried more, until the crying was uncontrollable. It was the first time I'd ever cried for my dead children.

Dear Father Joseph,

This is probably the hardest letter I will ever write in my life. I have told you everything that has happened in my life except one thing. I know that to be completely healed I must be honest. If you hate me after this, I won't blame you. I had an abortion when I was nineteen. An abortion! I took my child's life, not just once but twice. *Do you understand me? I took my children's lives.* I did not want to do this but I did it. There was a lot of pressure and I could not stand up to it. I hate myself. When you receive this and choose not to have anything to do with me again, I will understand.

Sincerely,
Liane

I walked away from the mailbox wishing I'd never mailed that letter. The secret was out. Someone knew. I held my breath for three days, fearing the worst. My hands trembled when I saw a letter from him in my post office box.

Dear Liane,

Just a note to say I got your letter. I'm writing to you in the hope you get this before you see me, so that you won't have to live with extra tension.

Four things

i) Thank you for your sharing—very brave of you.

ii) I don't judge people.

iii) On this journey called life, we all make mistakes, we all take wrong turns, we all do wrong.

iv) The way forward is not to beat ourselves up . . . but to try to understand why we do things we're ashamed of and then be gentle with ourselves.

Every good wish,
Joseph

I got down on my knees before God and wept. "Thank you, God, for Father Joseph, thank you for sending me such unconditional love." My whole life felt renewed because I was so accepted. I could feel God's healing love and it was painfully wonderful.

Down days followed, days when shame and guilt crowded out anything good. I sat with Father Joseph and could hardly talk. *Please listen to what I am not saying.*

He prayed with me, "Father, give Liane strength for this moment and healing for her lifetime."

With his encouragement, I began to meditate on God's forgiveness and believe that maybe I could forgive myself.

* * *

Now that my secret was told, I was ready for support. I joined Open Arms, a Protestant support group for women suffering from post-abortion stress. I learned that I was not crazy, that others had experienced the same mixed-up feelings and behaviors that I'd had. I was no longer alone.

After this group ended, I attended three weekends for adult children of alcoholics and survivors of childhood sexual abuse. This time I was with Catholics and, although my experience with the Protestant women had been good, the Catholic connection felt totally right. We were closer and more bonded because we shared the Sacraments and the Mass.

I began feeling better about myself. One day I realized the fog that surrounded me wasn't so dense any longer. I felt like my inner self was experiencing spring, even resurrection.

I sat in Father Joseph's office and tried to find words to explain to him what his reassurance and encouragement and belief in me meant. "Because of you I believe in myself. I can look at a picture of Jesus without shying away from it with guilt. I can read the Bible without feeling condemned, and new insights and meanings fill me. The voices of guilt and shame have stopped screaming at me."

He told me things about myself that I'd never heard before. "Liane, God had a special plan for you before you were conceived. He knew what your mission in life would be for Him, who you would meet on the way and who would help you to fulfill your mission."

Hearing him talk like that was painful, yet it was wonderful to be told that I was a Somebody when I'd always believed I was a nobody. For a few months I was in constant tears. Finally, I chose to believe what Father Joseph told me: that I was a special child of God. Page after page I wrote in my journal, *I am special. God does not make junk.*

Father Joseph encouraged me to look deeper into the Mass and understand its meaning and power and healing. Three phrases in particular spoke out to me.

> *I believe in the Holy Spirit, the Lord, the Giver of Life.* This Giver of Life did not desire me to live in death.

> *Lamb of God, you take away the sins of the world, have mercy on us. Lamb of God, you take away the sins of the world, grant us peace.* This told me that

Jesus, who had taken away my sins, would have mercy on me and would grant me peace in my heart.

Lord, I am not worthy to receive you, but only say the word and I shall be healed. Even though I was not worthy to receive Him, when I chose to accept the forgiveness I'd been hiding from all those years, I began to heal.

Daily through the Mass I changed rapidly, becoming more in love with God and life and myself each day.

Gradually I gained the strength to take my children and myself out of an abusive relationship. Leo and I are divorced, the marriage annulled and I am married to a fine man who treats us with respect and leads us in the way of life as a Catholic family.

I am reliving my childhood with my children, finding out how much fun a kid can really have. Now I put my arms around my children and tell them that I love them. We have frequent "Feelings Tea Parties" where we have tea and cookies or sandwiches and talk about feelings. I share with them that they, and all people, are special.

My life daily grows closer to Jesus, who heals me. He has brought me totally out of the fog and has given me new life.   My heart burns with love for the Eucharist. I feel an ever-increasing pull from Jesus to visit with him in the Blessed Sacrament.

My love for the Blessed Mother has greatly increased as I contemplate the life she gave to my Lord Jesus. Each day I become a saint to live a life worthy of Jesus. My life now is possible because I choose to believe that Jesus loves me and I am special. I believe this rather than ever listen to the voices of self-doubt that say I am a nobody.

I AM A SOMEBODY, loved by God, and he has wonderful plans for my life.

* * *

Editor's note: Liane Heron tells her story publicly in order to help others. She has started a support program in her archdiocese for women who seek healing of their abortions.

3

Days of Panic

Marie Teresa Patterson

✝

It was my birthday. The whole family had gone to Mass together as usual and Grandpa and Grandma had come over for one of Mom's special dinners. Dad and my brother, Stephen, told such funny stories we laughed and laughed. Afterwards we played games together. I have so many happy family memories . . .

During my growing up years I don't ever remember being a problem to anyone. Through high school I never rebelled against my parents or ever got into trouble. I rarely missed a CCD class. My interests were athletics, music and studies. Mostly I wanted to please people, especially my parents.

My picture from the yearbook shows a slender, attractive girl with long, blond hair and violet-blue eyes.   But the picture doesn't show how shy I was, too shy to find a boyfriend, although I longed for one.

Then, at the end of my sophomore year in college, I met Patrick. We shared a class and it was wonderful to have someone who was so easy to talk with. He, like me, was a runner. He was tall with brown hair and expressive dark eyes. Although we were both good students, Patrick was much more intense about studying and exceeding in competition.

We had great times together, sharing our interests, listening to each other's stories. It had been my dream for so long to have a friend. We went on bike trips, mountain picnics, boat rides. Ordinary outings were so much fun when we were together. Our major difference was religion. I was religious, a Catholic who believed in most of the Church's teachings. Patrick wasn't raised in any church at all.

Eventually the issue of sex came up. "Marie, what's wrong with making love if two people love each other?"

"I want to wait until I'm married to have sex. Sex makes two people one and should only be shared in marriage."

Patrick, not convinced, continued with his persuasion. "If you really loved me, you'd make love to me."

I resisted. In time we went our separate ways.

Then, two years later, when I was in graduate school, Patrick got a summer internship in the town where I was studying. Our friendship resumed. We were both on the edge of establishing careers and it was exciting to be together again and sharing our dreams. During that summer, against my better judgment and the values I had once stated, I let myself get pressured into sex.

Beforehand, I went to see a gynecologist. His advice was that contraceptive foam was reliable. I told myself, "It's all right, we love each other and we want to share our love." Yet I knew that wasn't true, and deep in my heart I felt guilty. Especially at Mass I wanted to hide from God.

Then, towards the end of summer, I realized I hadn't had my period for quite some time. I wasn't too concerned because as a runner I often didn't have my period for months. But Patrick was worried. So just to please him I got a home pregnancy test. It came up negative as I knew it would.

But Patrick was still worried, and so I agreed to a blood test. A few days later, during one of my graduate rotations, I was surprised to get a call from my gynecologist, "Marie, your blood test is positive."

I whispered into the phone, "Oh my God." My heart started racing and I felt my chest constrict. I started to shake.

The doctor tried to console me, "This doesn't have to be the end of the world; maybe you can get married."

But I was in such shock I hardly listened to him. I hung up the phone and tried to finish out the morning but my mind and body felt numb. Shaking, I called Patrick at work, "Meet me for lunch and I'll tell you the results of my test."

When we met we started walking. "You're pregnant, aren't you?"

"Yes."

"I knew it. I just knew it." He looked scared and I thought he was probably as scared as I was. "Well, I guess I'll have to marry you."

But I knew him. He wasn't ready to get married at that time. And I didn't want to marry him either.

At home that night, I needed to tell some-one what was happening in my life. But, who? I couldn't tell my parents. All I could think of was how disappointed they would be. So I called my sister, Janie. As soon as I heard her voice I started crying. "I . . . I'm . . . I'm pregnant." She tried to calm me down but I kept crying.

She asked, "Do you know what you're going to do?"

"I've been thinking about it all afternoon." I had already thought about abortion but I knew that it was murder. How could I ever make that choice? Yet when I thought about going through with the pregnancy and how eventually my parents would find out, and then what would they think of me, I couldn't bear it. Either choice scared me. Finally, I told Janie, "I guess I'm going through with the pregnancy."

"You're pretty brave."

I wasn't brave, though. I was really scared.

The next day I made an appointment to meet with a crisis pregnancy counselor. She said, "Whatever decision you make, you'll have to live with the rest of your life. If you have the baby you'll have the responsibility of taking care of it and providing for it. Are you emotionally ready to make that commitment?"

I felt myself growing unsteady inside.

She went on, "If you have an abortion, you'll have to live with that decision the rest of your life." I knew she was making me face the reality of the situation, but I left her office still scared and confused.

Next, I told a priest my story. He responded, "The Church teaches us to choose life, and an unborn baby is a life."

"But what if I did have an abortion?"

I felt the priest could see the terror in my eyes and could feel how scared I was. I felt he sympathized with my situation and the decision I had to make. He answered, "If you make the other decision, God will forgive you."

When I talked to Patrick again he said, "I wish you'd choose the abortion. Yesterday I told my mother and she agrees it would be best."

"Is that what you really want?"

"Going through a pregnancy would change both of our lives and I don't want this to happen." Then he said what I knew he'd say, "I'm not ready to get married and have a child."

All these responses left me confused. The more I listened to everyone, the worse I felt. I just wanted this whole thing to go away. I thought about how the counselor had asked if I was emotionally ready. I had told her that I wasn't and that I was scared. As the days went by, I hung onto that excuse. In the end, it seemed like reason enough to have an abortion.

I remember the day. It was 6:00 A.M. Friday and I walked the mile to the hospital by myself. This was the most terrifying day of my whole life, and I'd never felt so alone. Patrick's summer internship was over and even though he was flying in later, that was no help to me on my solitary journey.

At the hospital, I was taken to the day surgery room. Alone and numb I put on the gown. Alone and numb I followed directions. Alone and numb I waited. Alone and numb I was wheeled to the operating room. I don't remember anything else.

In the recovery room the anesthesia started to wear off and I began throwing up. The next thing I knew I was back in the day surgery and Patrick had arrived. "How do you feel?"

I didn't feel anything except relief that I wasn't pregnant and that no one had found out. I was so glad it was over.

The next day Patrick and I went for a bicycle ride. He said something unkind and I felt very emotional and upset over it. I responded, "How can you say that to me after what I've just been through?" After the weekend he wrote one letter and that was the end. I was alone again.

* * *

I resumed my training as a physical therapy student and totally disassociated myself from the abortion. When my sister and parents proudly came out for my graduation, it was as if the abortion had never happened.

After graduation I took a job as a physical therapist in Seattle. Although I didn't actually think of the abortion, I often felt ashamed at Mass like I wanted to hide from God.

In Seattle I didn't know anyone so every few weeks I went home to Portland to visit my parents. One evening my brother and I were having a good time playing a game and listening to the radio. There was a song on the radio that went something like this: "I am in the sky looking at you and I can read your mind . . ."

All of a sudden I started thinking about God looking down at me and how He really could read my mind. I couldn't stand to listen to that song. I jumped up from the game we were playing, got in my car and started driving. All the fun of the evening was gone. All I could think about was, God knows about the abortion. I thought I would never, never feel really happy again. Or if I did start to feel happy, the memory of what I'd done would surface and bring me down to the gray, joyless state that I was now experiencing.

Back in Seattle I couldn't stop thinking about what I'd done, that I'd sinned by having an abortion. I ended up in a face-to-face confession with one of the younger priests in my parish. It was the first time I'd told anyone except my sister, and I cried the whole time.

The priest was very gentle and kind, "I can tell you are truly sorry for what you've done." He gave me absolution. "God has forgiven you, but have you forgiven yourself?"

Kneeling in the church, I knew that God really had forgiven me. It was a great relief. I knew I wasn't going to have to hide from God anymore, and I could go to Mass and not feel ashamed.

But as for forgiving myself, how could I have done such a terrible thing? I was always the good one who did things right. Forgiving myself was a different story . . .

Meanwhile the years went by. I made some Christian friends and became involved in a women's Bible study. It was there that

Jesus became real to me and I grew to love Him in a personal way. Sometimes I felt unworthy of being in the study, but I would remind myself, "Marie, you're forgiven and Jesus wants you there."

Yet, television programs with anti-abortion protesters marching outside a clinic made me uneasy and anxious. I didn't want to hear about abortion. I always changed to another channel or else I'd snap the television off.

I started dating John, a man whom I really liked. We were on a picnic when the conversation came to children. He asked, "How many children would you like?"

That's when it all started.

After that conversation, I began to have panic and anxiety attacks. When they happened I could hardly breathe. My heart raced. I could barely move or talk. I felt like my life was oozing out of me. I didn't know what was happening. My hair would stand up and my scalp would tingle. My counselor tried to give me strategies to deal with the attacks but they didn't help enough. At night I couldn't sleep at all because of the tightness in my chest that wouldn't relax.

One afternoon in Portland I was feeling so anxious I didn't know if I was going to be able to drive home. My Dad and I were standing by my car, "Marie, what is it? There's something wrong, isn't there?" He looked at me with such compassion.

I was able to say, "Dad I've done something I feel really, really, bad about and I'm having a hard time forgiving myself. Do you think you could still love me?"

"What was it, hon?"

"I don't want to say it."

"It doesn't matter. I'll always love you, no matter what. Remember, you can go to God for forgiveness."

"I know, Dad." His affirmation helped. After our conversation, I was somehow able to get in the car and make it back to Seattle.

The attacks of anxiety kept on, and in the midst of them I wouldn't know what was happening to me. Driving became impossible. Meanwhile, my mother wanted me to come down to Portland for a visit because my brother was going to be there.

"I can't, Mom. I can't drive."

"Marie, honey, what's the matter? What's going on?"

I flew to Portland and she and I had a long talk. Her voice was full of love, "Why didn't you tell me sooner?"

"I was afraid of what you and Dad would think of me."

"I wish you'd come to us in the beginning. We would have supported you."

I remembered how all I'd thought about was that they'd be so ashamed. I'd never thought they would support me. If I'd known that I might have risked it.

"You know God has forgiven you."

"Yes."

"You have to forgive yourself."

"I don't know how."

Back in Seattle the panic attacks grew worse. I was more scared all the time. Also, I felt depressed. Would the panic and anxiety ever go away? Or would I live with this inability to function normally for the rest of my life?

A friend from work grew worried about me and he helped me make contact with a psychiatrist. The psychiatrist, who became like an understanding father to me, prescribed a drug called Xanax and gave me information to read about panic and anxiety disorder. As the sessions continued, the symptoms became less and less.

I began to understand how during all those years since the abortion I'd been using enormous amounts of energy trying to keep the abortion below the surface. What looked like a normal life was really an exhausting battle to keep what I'd done out of my conscious mind. After John's questions about children, I panicked when I couldn't keep it pushed down any longer.

Understanding myself helped. The Xanax which I took whenever I felt any slight panic helped, too. It gave me some control.

But I still needed help. Then, like an answer to prayer, a friend told me about Heart to Heart, a Christian-based support group/Bible study for post-aborted women. I joined a group and went to the meetings for two-and-a-half hours every Tuesday night for eight weeks.

The first night was very emotional. The leader and co-leader and four other women like myself shared our stories and cried for ourselves and each other. The leader said, "You may not believe this now, but after these eight weeks you will come to a point much further along in your healing process where you will not only feel better but feel joy again."

I could hardly believe I'd ever feel really happy again. But the first things I learned were two promises from God:

He will turn your mourning into dancing. (Psalm 30:11.)

He will not remember the shame of your youth. (Isaiah 43:25)

These scriptures filled me with hope for the future.

We worked through the stages of grief including relief, denial, repentance, anger, depression, forgiveness, acceptance and letting go.

Even though I knew God had forgiven me, I became aware of my inwardly-directed anger. I hadn't forgiven myself and that was another one of the reasons I was depressed. I wrote about this in my journal:

> I'm angry at myself for getting together with Patrick again. I hate how I let him use me and manipulate my emotions. I hate how I tried to please him. I'm angry over my decision to have the abortion and that I didn't speak to the right people. I'm angry that I was so weak. How could I have been so naive?

Somedays the only thing that helped me was reading the Bible and personalizing God's promises:

> "By his wounds I, Marie, am healed."
> (1 Peter 2: 21-25)

> "I, Marie, am in Christ and I am a new creation." (2 Corinthians 5:17)

Those Scriptures and others like them were powerful as they helped me to realize that even though I had messed up, God could give me a new life.

I also faced my anger at Patrick. I wrote about it as part of the homework:

> Patrick: I despise what you did to me. You were a selfish, immature, insecure person. I wanted to please you and you misled me. I look back and it makes me sick. You disgust me. I'm so angry at you I can't stand to look at your picture or write your name. All you thought of was yourself. You left me feeling so empty and so hurt. I take responsibility for the part I played but you are very much to blame.

One of the most significant areas of my sessions with the psychiatrist was the time we spent discussing this anger at myself and Patrick. Gradually, through his counsel, I began to understand where Patrick was coming from and I grew in compassion for the person he had been then. At Heart to Heart, I saw in the Scriptures that God really wanted me to forgive. Through all of this I was at last able to write in my journal:

> Dear Patrick, I'm not mad at you anymore. I don't like a lot of the things you did to me, manipulation of my emotions, the way you made me feel. But I forgive you for the part you played in my abortion. You were raised

in a family that didn't believe in the
Lord, or didn't know him. You didn't
know the truth. I pray the Lord will
send Christians into your life to lead
you to Him. I also forgive your mother
and pray that she will find the Lord
someday, too . . .

It was deeply healing to my inner self to
let go of the anger and forgive the past. But
even harder than forgiving Patrick was forgiving myself. I'd asked myself a thousand
times how I could have done what I did?
But with the counsel of the psychiatrist and
the support of the Bible study, I began to
see the person whom I had been then. As I
did, I was able to grow in compassion for
myself. I wrote:

Dear Marie, you don't deserve to torture
yourself forever with unforgiveness.
You need to forgive that young, naive,
scared girl. Back then you longed to be
in love so much that you compromised
your beliefs. You tried to justify what
you did but you had no idea of the
cost. You made a big mistake but you
must stop trying to make yourself suffer for what you did. Jesus paid the
cost. As you accept this, forgive yourself. Jesus doesn't want you to suffer.
He wants you to be joyful in being forgiven and doing his will.

Now that compassion and forgiveness for myself had begun, I was able to write a letter to my child.

> Dear Jamie, That is the name I chose for you. I ask your forgiveness for what I did. I'm so, so sorry. Please forgive me, I'm not the same person now that I was then. What keeps me going is Jesus' love for me and my desire to follow him and be with Him someday and united with you. Until then you will always hold a special place in my heart. I love you. Someday I will see you and tell you myself.
>
> Love,
>
> Mommy

In our eight-week session, the final stage was acceptance and letting go. These were the most important steps, we were told, because they helped us get on with our lives. I wrote a letting-go prayer to Jesus.

> Lord, this is very hard for me to do but I give my baby to you and to your care. And I let go of the past. I want to serve you and do your will. Help me to finally be free and able to be used by you. Amen.

What happened next was that the Lord did use me. I met a Catholic woman named Liane who was also post-aborted. We started a small support group for Catholic women who had had abortions. We talked about issues which were specifically Catholic and shared our Catholic experience concerning abortions, especially the guilt.

On June 3, 1992, seven years after Jamie died, my friend, Irene, who was mourning the abortion of her grandchild, and I attended a memorial Mass that a priest friend, Fr. Joseph, said for our two babies.

Following the readings Father led us in a meditation.

I saw myself in a valley, sitting under a tree, near a river. It was sunny and I got up and began to hike up a foothill to a mountain. At the top it was very peaceful and in the distance I could see Jesus walking towards me. When he came closer I saw how gentle and loving his eyes were. They seemed to look right through my soul. I knew deep within me that He loved me and that I was forgiven and that I needed to get on with my life.

I came down the mountain and there by a pool was my little girl. She was bright and beautiful with long, dark hair, pulled back from her face. She was smiling. I stood with her in my arms. Then I reached into the pool and splashed water on her head twice and baptized her.

I carried her back up the mountain. Jesus walked towards us and I saw his loving eyes again. I gave him Jamie. He took her and started walking away. It was sad to give her up but I knew that she was safe and happy and where we all want to be someday.

After this meditation Father Joseph continued the Mass. At the end he said that whenever we are in the presence of God, especially during Mass, we could be united with our children again. In closing, Irene and I each put a rose, a symbol of our children's brief lives, next to a statue of the Blessed Virgin, our heavenly mother.

Since then my father has died. I think of him almost every day and hope that he has met his granddaughter, Jamie. At night I ask Jesus to tell them both how much I love them.

Today I am well. No more panic attacks and anxiety. I do feel happy, and memories of the abortion do not drag me down. But I know that right now there are many thousands of women who feel like I did and I want to say to each one: don't try to figure out your anger and pain and depression by yourself. Reach out for help and you will find that you are not alone.

National Office of Post-Abortion Reconciliation & Healing Support Referral Line: 1-800-5WE-CARE

4

Keeper of Rules

Liz Young-Arbol

✝

"Father, forgive me for I have sinned. It's been six weeks since my last confession. I've been using birth control . . ."

The year was 1965. I was 25, raising two children (Debbie, two, and Billy, four) while my husband, Don, was in the Navy. While he had been home for three weeks, we had used birth control. Now he was back at sea. I was brokenhearted over my sin. I loved God. I loved the Church. I didn't want to break the rules. In the confessional after confessing my sin, I explained my future dilemma.

"I know that using birth control is a mortal sin, but the way things are, I have to practice it when my husband comes back from Vietnam. He'll only be in port for two or three weeks. So as much as I'd love to go to Mass and Communion while he's gone, I can't because I can't promise not to use birth control when he comes home. Just to go to Mass without receiving Communion doesn't make sense and to not go to Mass is a mortal sin. So, Father, what am I going to do? I've always wanted to and tried to keep the rules and now I can't."

"Child, how long until your husband returns?" The half-whispered voice from the other side of the confessional partition sounded compassionate.

"Over a year."

"Now you don't even know if he'll come back from Vietnam alive. When and if he does, you might feel differently about more children. Why not face the issue when he returns? If he returns."

It sounded reasonable. "Yes, I guess I can do that."

That night Billy, Debbie and I sat around the kitchen table for a lonely meal of sandwiches. Halfway through, Billy started whining. "I miss Daddy. I wish he could come home. When Daddy's home, we have a good dinner."

"I want Daddy, too." Debbie echoed her brother in the same whining voice.

They kept it up until my nerves felt frazzled. "Stop it, both of you. Your Daddy's gone and that's the way it is." My voice was way too cross, but I couldn't seem to help it.

Billy started crying. Then his milk spilled. The table was a sea of white, cascading into my lap. "Now look what you've done," I yelled. Debbie started crying, too. It was too much for me. I slapped Billy. "Get out of here, both of you. Go to your room." They left sobbing.

I wept and prayed as I cleaned up the milk. "Dear God, what a terrible mother I am. I'm not cut out to be a single parent. I'm too cross. It's too hard."

Later, after I had let Billy and Debbie stay up way too late to make up for my anger, I reflected on the priest's advice. Even though I loved my children, I knew another child would be too much for me to handle emotionally. Yes, I could do what the priest said, face the birth control issue when Don came home and go to Mass and Communion now, but I had nagging doubts about that really being right. I already knew what I would have to do when Don returned.

1966. Don was coming home for six weeks. I'd loved going to Mass and Communion when he was gone and I didn't want this to change. So I went to confession to a different priest, hoping he would tell me that under these conditions it was all right to practice birth control. The advice from beyond the confessional window broke my heart. "If you want to stay in the state of grace to receive Holy Communion, then you and your husband must live like brother and sister."

I was a healthy young woman, in love with my husband who had been gone a year. The advice was unthinkable. I welcomed Don home with all my heart. We used birth control and, to my sorrow, I stayed away from Mass.

By the time we were transferred to Japan, the pattern was set. When Don was at sea, which was most of the time, I played the rationalization game. "Liz, you don't know that the ship won't be hit," and I went to Mass and Communion, often daily. When the ship came in, I didn't go to Mass. I only broke the rules because I had to. I didn't want to.

When Don came home, we used condoms or foam. But sex wasn't spontaneous with this kind of birth control and sometimes we used nothing. Once more I was pregnant.

The afternoon that the dispensary called with the positive results of the pregnancy test, Don's ship was coming in. I stood on the dock with the other wives, waiting. This day I needed him desperately, and I counted the minutes until I could feel his arms around me. Then, before our very eyes, the ship turned around at the breakwater and went back to sea.

With that, my whole situation seemed more than I could bear. The week before, the Pueblo had been captured and now the rumor had it that Don's ship was going to get her back. I had no idea when he would return. I was living far from home with the penetrating weariness and loneliness of a different culture. I had no relief from the children, and I was growing less loving every day, using a belt to spank them and raising welts. And now I was pregnant. I felt desperately, desperately afraid.

It was six long, long weeks before Don returned. After we made love, I told him the decision I'd made about my pregnancy. "I have to have an abortion."

"Liz, honey, there's always room for one more child."

"You don't understand. There isn't."

"But abortion isn't legal."

"Not in the United States. But here in Japan it is."

"If you have complications and go to a Navy hospital, we'll both be in trouble."

"Don, listen to me. You go off to sea, how do you know there's always room for one more? You're never here. What do you know about the struggle I face? What do you know about how I want to be a loving mother and yet I know that I'm not?"

"But, honey . . ."

"I can't go though with it, Don. I've made up my mind."

Still I prayed, "Please, God, let me have a miscarriage. I don't want to commit the sin of abortion. I don't want to go against You or your Church or the rules." Yet another side of me thought, maybe abortion is the perfect solution. I could go to Mass and Communion and not worry about birth control. After all, I might not get pregnant. And if I did, I could get an abortion because, unlike birth control, it was a one-time sin.

When my ongoing struggle to do what was right met head-on with my ongoing agony over being pregnant again, this rationalizing didn't seem strange. Another thing, I'd had conversations with other Navy wives about abortion and the enormity of the act was never discussed.

After Don returned to sea, my friend, Lillian, drove me to the abortionist and interpreted for me. By this time I was four months pregnant. I have no memories of the abortion because I was completely put out. But as I came to, I could hear Lillian's voice discussing it with her husband, "It was terrible. The doctor made me witness it. I saw the baby, its hands and arms and body. It was a boy." She cried and told him again and again what she'd seen. As I laid there in that tiny space, with the curtains enclosing me in with the voice of my hysterical friend, suddenly the reality was too big, too horrible to ever be rationalized away.

The truth lay like a crushing weight on my conscience. I was a murderer.

I wrote to Don and told him I was no longer pregnant. Then I called the chapel to find out which chaplain was hearing confessions, and picked the Saturday that Father Hamilton was hearing. I went to confession knowing and fully believing that even though I had sinned deliberately and taken a life, God would forgive me and my sin would go away with the words of absolution.

Father was kind and understanding but I walked out of the confessional feeling guiltier than ever.

I went to bed every night knowing that I was a murderer, and woke up each morning with the same knowledge.

It was a worse agony than being pregnant ever was. One of my reasons for getting the abortion was that another child would make me less loving than I was to my children. But now I was so short-tempered with them I had to get away from them. What's more, I had to get away from me. I threw myself into volunteer work. I joined the Navy Wives' Club. I got a job. I went to Mass daily. Every single Saturday I went to confession, and confessed to God that I was a murderer. Even though the chaplain explained God's forgiveness, I absolutely knew I wasn't forgiven.

When Don's ship came in, nothing was the same between us. He was cool towards me and I felt wounded by his rejection. I initiated much of our sexual activity so I could feel okay, without birth control so I wouldn't sin again. A week passed and he returned to sea. Was I pregnant? I was so afraid, so scared and torn and angry with everyone. At last my period came.

I couldn't go though that again.   The next time Don came home I went back to using birth control and stayed away from Mass.

I changed.   Once I'd lived close to God's love.   Now it seemed far away.   I put a defensive wall around me.   I constantly avoided babies.   I couldn't be in the same room with a baby without breaking into a cold sweat.   A baby's cry sent me running, and the words "murderer, murderer" swam in my head for weeks.

1968.   Two years after the abortion, Don had gone back to sea again when the dispensary called, "Liz, the tests show you're pregnant."

No, no, no, no, no.   I sat by the phone and wept.   Then slowly I picked up the phone to schedule an abortion.   But before the call could go through, I hung up the receiver.   I knew the enormity of abortion.   I couldn't do it again.

Instead I did everything in my power to cause a miscarriage.   If I miscarried, it would not be a sin.   One Saturday afternoon, after lifting heavy furniture and douching with scalding water I went to Mass to pray that what I had done would succeed in the much-wanted miscarriage.

I got there early and shortly after, the chaplain came out of the sacristy with a couple. He was going to baptize their baby. I broke into a cold sweat. I knew that when the priest poured the water, the baby would cry and I would scream. There was no way out of the chapel without being noticed. All I could do was stay and keep my fists clenched and my teeth gritted. Afterwards I went home and cried all night.

I knew that God was not going to give me the miscarriage. I thought it was because He had not forgiven the abortion. I turned to bargaining. "God, if you will just forgive me, I'll go to Mass everyday and teach CCD for the rest of my life. I'll be a loving mother and wife and never yell again." Instead of growing close to God like I deeply desired, I became a religious nut. I started teaching CCD and doing everything at the chapel in order to punish myself so that God would forgive me. But I was still a murderer. That just wouldn't go away.

1969. The baby, Frankie, was born. I could not hold him without shaking. I only carried him in an infant seat. Debbie, almost seven, held him and played with him. The maid Don had hired to placate me fed and bathed him. I didn't bond with him and my bonding with Debbie and Billy practically ceased.

1971. We came back to the States and I had my tubes tied. I didn't think about it. I just did it to survive. I still went to confession and confessed the abortion but not as much. I kept my bargain with God, continuing my punishment of going to daily Mass and teaching CCD. But this punishment wasn't enough to make me feel forgiven. I still woke up in cold sweats. The words, "murderer, murderer" still swam in my head. I needed further punishment. I talked Don into taking in unwed mothers. Abortion now was legal, and I could spare someone the anguish I lived with.

1974. Another dilemma. I enjoyed sharing my home and my life with the unwed mothers. I loved teaching CCD so much that I landed a part-time job as parish Director of Religious Education (DRE). My punishments weren't punishments anymore. I had almost quit confessing the abortion and now I started confessing it over and over again.

By now Billy was 13, Debbie was 11 and Frankie was 5. These should have been happy years. We were settled in the States. My work was meaningful. The children were growing. Instead, whenever I was alone I cried. One afternoon, coming home from work, I cried so hard I couldn't see the road. I pulled off and great sobs shook my body. Murderers go to jail. Why didn't someone send me to jail? I had to find another punishment.

But before I could decide on how to further punish myself, something else happened. I went to a lecture for DRE's on sin and morality. The lecturing priest used abortion as an example of premeditated, deliberate sin. Though he probably didn't say it, I heard unforgivable. I sat through it and seethed. What did he know about the anguish of a woman pregnant and alone and terrified?

After the lecture I approached him in a white-hot rage. "You are the most pompous, self-satisfied excuse for a priest I've ever seen. You're critical, judging, condemning, without a shred of compassion, without a notion of love." I began to cry. With tears pouring down my face, I told him I'd had an abortion.

He asked me to make an appintment with him. He listened intently to my whole story. "Liz, do you think you need to forgive yourself? God has forgiven you and He loves you. You don't need to punish yourself. If teaching CCD is punishment, that's the wrong reason to teach." He suggested that I go for counseling. The door to sanity opened a little that day.

At home I asked Don if he would consider going to counseling. I didn't say why because neither of us ever spoke of the abortion.

"No way, Liz. Crazy people need counseling. Not me. Certainly not us."

I don't know why I let the door close on counseling. But I did. Instead I began to spend huge amounts of money, buying things we couldn't afford. But having nice things didn't make me feel good about myself. I only felt guiltier.

1976. The Church began teaching that penance was supposed to be meaningful. Okay. I could give my punishment meaning. I gave up spending. I wouldn't buy myself *anything*. I let my hair go so people could tell by looking at me that I was a terrible person. This also kept people at a distance; no one could become my friend and then drop me when they got to know me.

1977. One of the women in the parish worked with Human Life, giving speeches on the sanctity of life. I simply could not go and hear her speak. Finally, over lunch I said, "You must be wondering why I don't come and listen to you talk. Eleven years ago I had an abortion, and I'm afraid your speech would send me into a tailspin."

Her eyes met mine. "I can understand that."

I'd expected disgust, condemnation, perhaps even the loss of my job. Instead I received friendship. She invited me to her house. I was perplexed. She and her husband treated me as if I'd never had an abortion, as if I was a good person. It helped in a way I can't even explain.

This came at a good time because my marriage to Don, which had never been the same since the abortion, was going downhill. By this time he hadn't touched me for a year.

1978. Don died of cancer without ever forgiving me.

1979. During a doctrinal program in ministry, I took a class on personal alienation. Sitting around the table (only two of the ten were women), the topic came to the fallout of abortion. As my colleagues began to discuss it, I started to cry. Humiliated, I jumped up and ran out of the room. It had been 13 years since the abortion. Yet whenever that word came up, it would pull off the scab and I would begin to bleed.

1980. Dear God, will I ever be healed? My friend became a grandmother and, in an attempt to get me unstuck from my fears, she put her granddaughter in my arms. I held the baby only three minutes before I began to shake.

1981-1986. Terrible years dealing with teen-age alcoholism and drug abuse. I was in such emotional overload I couldn't even think about the abortion, let alone deal with it. I just kept myself far away from babies.

1987. Billy, who had completed an alcohol recovery program, was married. His wife was pregnant and so was Debbie. Two new babies I wouldn't be able to avoid. I went before God and pleaded, "Please let me hold them without trembling, or crying, or running out of the room. I'll do anything. Just get me through it."

I was there for Billy's wife's delivery, simply because there was no way out of it. My first grandchild was minutes old when Billy put him in my arms. I didn't shake. The baby cried. I didn't sweat or scream. God had answered my prayers. I could be a grandmother!

1990. Having grandchildren opened the door at last. It was time to do something positive about all my guilt. A priest, Fr. Joseph, put me in touch with Liane, another woman who had had an abortion. Together we went to Open Arms, a Christian support group for women who have had abortions.

Open Arms helped me honestly face what I had done. Yes, I had taken the life of my child. But I was helped to put my choice in some sort of perspective. Because the leaders had "been there" and had experienced the loving, healing touch of Jesus, they were able to lead me to the healing fountain of His love and mercy.

But to do so required hard work and brutal honesty. I acknowledged my hidden anger; anger at myself for not being a stronger person, anger at Don for leaving me in a foreign country, for being at sea and for being no help in raising Debbie and Billy, anger at a Church that did not seem to understand the dilemma of women who wanted to follow the rules but could make no sense of them.

Each week we looked at Scripture to see how it might help us to see our lives more clearly. We shared our stories with other women. Weekly we completed homework assignments. Part of the process was to spend time writing about what had happened and answering questions regarding our relationships with husbands, selves, friends and church.

At last I was ready to face myself. It was Memorial Day. My present husband was playing golf and Frankie was gone for the holiday weekend. I knew that if I stopped to get something to eat or drink I would never return to the writing, so I prepared ahead of time.

In the kitchen, I fixed myself a tray of every goody in the house, found a spiral notebook and a few pens. In the bedroom I put on my most comfortable pajamas, crawled into bed and began to write.

Once I started to write, the pen flowed and so did the tears. I wrote and cried for several hours. The tears were different than any of the tears I had shed before, they were more like the tears one cries in compassion for someone else. All the while I was writing I could feel the loving and healing presence of God.

God also showed me my abuse toward the older children. Even though I knew I had not always been loving, it was the first time I had ever acknowledged that I had been an abusive mother, and I asked forgiveness for that part of my life, too.

Once I was finished with the writing, I felt drained and euphoric at the same time. It was if a great weight had been lifted off my shoulders. I no longer needed to carry all of that awfulness around in my heart. It was all safely written down in my journal, and now there was room inside of me to be open to experience whatever else God might have in store for me.

I somehow knew that the work was not complete. While I felt somewhat better, there was something else that needed to happen for me to feel healed. I knew that I had at last accepted God's forgiveness and I had forgiven myself. So what else was left?

The leader talked about bringing some sort of closure to the abortion event. Since I knew the child was a boy, I named him Justin because that was a name that Don had liked. My friend, Liane, suggested that I pray to our Blessed Lady for an answer about what to do. Well, I just wasn't too sure about that. I had been turned off about Mary for years. She seemed plastic and not at all real. My mother had a great devotion to her and it always seemed to me that she was copping out. To me the adult thing to do was go straight to God. That's where our prayers ended up anyway, wasn't it? Besides, how could someone who was conceived without sin, had never sinned, and had devoted her whole life to the will of God ever understand what a mother and wife faces in today's world? But since I wasn't coming up with any other answers, I decided to try Liane's suggestion. What did I have to lose?

However, even though as part of my job as DRE I teach prayer, I didn't have an idea of how to go about this prayer. Did I get down on my knees? Did I pray in church? Should I start with the rosary? (If so, I would have to buy one!) Did I need to be apologetic to Our Lady, saying something like, "I'm sorry I negated your power for so many years, but could you help me just this once?"

After a few days of playing with scenarios in my mind, I finally found some quiet time. In the quietness of my room, while laying in bed, I closed my eyes and pictured myself knocking on Mary's door. She answered my knock and I asked if could speak to her.

She invited me into her home. I was surprised! It looked like an ordinary, modern home of the 80s. We sat down at the kitchen table, and over a cup of tea I asked her if she would find Don.

She reached out and covered my hand with hers. I talked fast so I would not lose my nerve. She said she would find him.

Then I asked her, "When you find him, would you ask him to find Justin? If he can't find Justin, would you find him? Would you ask Don to tell Justin how sorry I am that he had not been given a chance at life? And ask Don to place Justin at the feet of Jesus, and ask Jesus to bless him and heal any hurt he experienced because his mother had aborted him?"

Mary said she would.

I gave her a hug and hurried away. Shortly after that prayer (a week or so) I realized a peacefulness. I can't tell you the day or the hour it happened, but it was just there one day. Then, in a dream, I saw Don with Justin in the presence of Jesus.

Towards the end of the Open Arms sessions, one of the women was selling some very small dolls. I bought one. The doll stands for Justin. In my sewing room there is a corner where the doll sits on a glass shelf. Next to the shelf are some flowers and this quote:

> Forgiveness is the fragrance the violet
> sheds on the foot that crushes it.

Very few people know what that corner is all about. They comment on the flowers or the cute doll. But the corner is a place where I can go when I feel sad or unforgiven. It is there to remind me in a positive way of a child who did not have a chance to live. It is there to remind me that forgiveness is the greatest gift I can give myself. It is there to remind me that forgiveness from God is always available. I only have to ask.

5

Journey

Heidi Maria Schmidt

⚓

Today I remember the one I killed. I tried for years not to think about her, and almost succeeded. In fact I almost succeeded in destroying all that's good in life. I will tell you her short little story and, in telling it, I will tell you mine . . .

I grew up in a large family with four brothers and one sister. I was the youngest. We were a boisterous family, all of us blond with strong German features. Every morning Mama plaited my sister's and my hair into thick, long braids. We were involved in swimming and music, faithful attendees at Mass and CCD, for all appearances quite normal. But under the surface, things were far from the way they looked.

Despite our family activities, we all walked on eggshells around Papa. He was unpredictable. One moment he was charming, and then off he'd go into a violent display of temper. Laziness, waste, ungratefulness all set him off. Mama was his target most often, and he ripped her to shreds with bitter, hard-hitting sarcasm and sheer profanity.

I remember when she made a mistake in the family bookkeeping. That was the signal that day that caused him to rampage through the house. He was a terrifying sight, all red-faced with bulging veins. "Damn you, Ella, can't you do anything right? I've told you a thousand times to keep track of the expenses. You know how I hate wastefulness and incompetency, and yet you can't be bothered." He was just getting started.

When I was six or seven, I played outside before I cleaned my room. He went into a rage. I stood in the middle of the kitchen while he screamed at me. "You stupid little brat. How many times do I have to tell you something before you get it through your stupid head?" The more he shouted, the bigger he seemed to get and the smaller I felt. By the time he'd vented his anger, there was nothing left of me at all.

What made Papa's anger so hard to bear was that I loved him. Often I rubbed his neck after work and sat on his lap while he read the paper. He sang with us and encouraged us to study. He thought I was bright and he had so many dreams for me.

But because of his unpredictability it was difficult to trust him. When I told him things, he often used them against me and that made it impossible to look to him for protection.

So when, at three years of age, my older brothers started involving me in sexually-orientated games, I naturally did not breathe a word of it to Papa. Because I was so young when they started, I can't ever remember a time when I was truly innocent, without some knowledge of my own sexuality.

At first I didn't realize what I was doing was wrong. The games were on the sly, yes, but it was normal to hide everyday things from Papa. But as I grew older and understood, I faced my brothers. "No, I'm not doing it anymore."

"You better or we're telling Papa that you touch your private parts." That was all the threat I needed to keep quiet and comply.

I understand now that what happened to me at home was the reason I was not able to make friends well. I let myself be picked on and slighted. Then I cried from loneliness.

I was twelve before I could say a firm NO to my brothers. At last they backed off. But I was left with a precocious awareness of self and no firmly-set boundaries that led me into trouble as a teen.

Any innocence I had left was destroyed by another event. When I was in the eighth grade, I chose my oldest brother's new wife for my Confirmation sponsor. It was sort of a welcome-to-the-family gesture, even though she was not an outstanding Catholic role model. While I was at her house I discovered the book, *The Wolf and the Dove*. It was a classic soft porn novel, and she permitted me to read it. I read scenes I never should have known about. This gave me some further mixed-up ideas on correct sexual behavior and relationships, as well as putting some attractively perverse ideas in my head.

Despite this, my Confirmation was an important day to me. As I stood in line to approach the bishop, my heart yearned for God.

But at the same time I desperately sought affection in intimacy. I began dating early and was fully sexually active by the age of

15. Sex was a payoff. In exchange for favors, I heard kind words and I was held.

Yet I knew that God was calling to me to change my life. Through youth rallies and retreats I prayed fervently and longed to live by God's ways. One night after a Catholic youth meeting, a boy brought me home. We were innocently snuggled on the sofa and talking about the meeting when my father walked in. He burst into one of his rages, "Heidi, get yourself in the kitchen." He started screaming before the door was closed. "You dirty slut, sitting there with that boy. All he wants to do is get in your pants. Don't you know what effect you have on boys by rubbing your breasts all over them?"

I was deeply humiliated and I fled the house with the boy. We ended up parking and going too far.

My life became so mixed up. I wanted to feel valued and I found it with the affection and intimacy of sex. But I wanted God, too. I tried to have both by telling myself that as long as two people agreed, then no one was hurt.

But I did get hurt. I fell in love with Robin. His family was wonderful to me and treated me with far more love and respect than I'd ever known at home. With the joy of his family's acceptance, I had dreams of marrying Robin and being really valued and happy.

We had sex twice, and to me that seemed like holding back. Then the night of our senior prom, Robin and I attended Mass together. The priest preached on the benefits of saying no to sex outside of marriage and why we should respect each other. Robin turned to me and said, "I would have loved you more if you had said no." *He was blaming me for what he had wanted to do, too.* I felt like he'd stabbed me.

Later that night he broke up with me. I ached with the pain of rejection and loss. I had really loved him.

In the fall I went away to nursing school. One of the students, Tommy, from a poor family, fell in love with me. I taught him how to eat in restaurants, how to dress and . . . how to love. In return he gave me the affection I craved. Meanwhile, he'd asked my parents to be his sponsors for Baptism and Confirmation. They were proud to sponsor him into the Church.

But Tommy didn't value me the way I needed to be valued. Just as I decided to break up with him, I found out I was pregnant. This was a terrible time of not knowing what to do and struggling with constant morning sickness and a full load of studies.

Tommy, however, was so pleased with the pregnancy he acted like the first man to ever impregnate a woman. While my parents were celebrating his Baptism and Confirmation, he gave them the news: "Heidi's pregnant and we're going to be married."

I could only cower while Papa raged, "All your life you've done nothing but humiliate me. I've tried and I've tried but you deliberately disobey me." Mama cried and said nothing at all.

The marriage was planned but without any joy. Then, during the pre-Cana classes, I just knew that I couldn't marry Tommy. When I told him, he left and went a thousand miles away, leaving me to face my father's wrath alone. "Heidi, do you realize how ashamed we are? Don't you know your mother cries herself to sleep every night? I don't know how much more we can take. We are so embarrassed by you, we don't want you to come to our parish anymore."

I did as they asked. I sat alone in another church.

When the new semester began at nursing school, I found I was cut off from the money Papa had promised. I was broke and hungry before the school helped me out. Then some classmates got a petition against me to prevent the school from helping me. Even though the school threw out the petition, I felt hurt and betrayed by the people I'd thought would support me. As the baby grew inside me, I felt more desperate every day.

I gave birth to a little girl I named Lisa. Even though my heart broke inside me, I had to place her for adoption. But for the five days I had her, I fought to be able to hold her and even forced the hospital to break the rules so I could be with her. When I put my little daughter in the case-worker's arms, I knew she would disappear from my life forever.

The chaplain came and heard my confession and gave me Communion. He put his hand on my head, "Dear God, please give Heidi the grace she needs to make it through." The chaplain's support meant everything to me. It put me back in touch with the love that I knew God had for me.

But giving up my little daughter wounded me. I didn't want to let her go. I only parted with her so she would have everything she needed to grow. I headed for home hurt and angry over the sacrifice I'd had to make.

I was there for a day when the one class-
mate who had been a wonderful support
during my pregnancy came to visit. He sat
with me, his arm around my shoulder.
"Heidi, how are you really doing?"

"I hurt so bad I want to die."

My father stomped into the room, grabbed
me by the shoulder and dragged me out.
"You dirty little s___. How long before you
get knocked up with *this* man's child?"

Pain. So much pain. School had not been
a friendly place but I returned to it the next
day.

* * *

Soon I was dating a new man. Paul delighted in bringing me flowers and treats,
taking me to fine restaurants. He loved me
and I hungered for the intimacy that sex
brought. But my mood was fickle. When I
had a chance to see an old friend, Jim, who
was so much more romantic than Paul, I
decided I would rather be with him. Paul
and I had one last date, an out-of-town
wedding, and while I was drunk we slept together.

In five weeks I was throwing up each
morning. One of my friends, Angie, heard
the retching. "Heidi, are you pregnant?"

"Yes."

"Come to an abortion clinic that I know of. You don't have to go through this again."

I was a nursing student. I knew exactly what an abortion was. How could I take the life of my unborn child? How could I tell the school? How could I tell my parents? How could I manage without health insurance? How could I ever go through the pain of giving up another child for adoption? There was another consideration, too. Not only did I not love Paul, I didn't want to lose Jim.

I made my decision. "Paul, I have to have half the money for an abortion."

He was shocked. "Please don't have an abortion. This is my first conceived child. Please, Heidi, I love you. I want to marry you."

I wouldn't listen.

Angie went with me to the clinic and we had to walk past picketers. Gently they asked, "Can we help you stay pregnant?" They placed a phone number in my hand.

Defensively I retorted, "People come here for birth control and physical exams, too."

I had to see a clinic psychologist before they would do an abortion. He asked, "Have you considered all the options?"

"Yes, it's either this baby or me." I felt I couldn't face the rejection of my family or fellow students. If they treated me so badly when I was engaged, how would they treat me now that I was alone, without even a love relationship to justify my pregnancy?

I tried to be calm for the abortion. I brought music to listen to and I felt totally in control. But my tight control dissolved when I saw the doctor walk away with a suction canister, and I saw in all that blood, two little feet. Two little baby feet. I was screaming inside myself. "I'm sorry, baby." But it was too late. I went to my friend's house and spent the weekend mixing Valiums and alcohol and crying over what I had done.

The next week I went to confession. The priest was matter-of-fact, "Have nothing to do with abortions. From now on, try to discourage people from having abortions." I knew he didn't understand the guilt and pain that was cutting through my heart like a scalpel. I walked away with a heavy heart, feeling completely unforgiven.

Paul called again. "I'm going to kill myself. I can't live with what you've done."

I alerted the police as soon as he hung up. Fortunately his chosen method of suicide did nothing but give him a headache and get him locked up overnight in a psyche ward.

A month later he called me. "I'm sleeping with as many girls as possible." What had I done? He was a good man when I met him: respectful, kind, caring, a virgin, honorable. . . .

It was getting harder to pretend everything was okay. I started smoking and I gained 40 pounds during my senior year. As a nursing student I spent hours working in the newborn nursery. I rarely saw Jim, the man I'd thought was so important. Sometimes at night I lay awake and wondered what would have happened if I'd accepted the help of the picketers. If I had . . . but that was the agony. It could never be undone.

Finally I graduated and got a job as an OB nurse across the country. I moved in with three other girls, wilder than I was, and our wild living seemed to numb the pain of those two little feet. We read porno magazines and I watched my first X-rated video. I drugged my conscience into a deep sleep with alcohol and sexual relationships. I know now that I was looking for someone to value me, but none of the men I dated came close to meeting my neediness. Because I was so lonely, one of the girls introduced me to her cousin Danny. He was not a good influence.

Meanwhile, I met a really good and moral man, Eric. We talked for hours. He told me that God valued me and loved me.

"Me? How could that be true after what I've done?"

"He loves you and He died for you."

Finally Eric convinced me that Danny was not good for me. But unfortunately, by this time, I was already pregnant.

Danny's solution was an abortion. But I couldn't do that again and I couldn't give up another child, never to see or hear from her. Single parenting was my only option. I dreaded writing my parents with the news but they would have to know.

A curt reply followed:

> Heidi, under no circumstances do we feel you are ready to become a parent. If you keep the child, do not plan on us helping you in any way. You and the child will not be welcome in this house . . .

What on earth was I going to do?

Through counseling, through the support of my coworkers, through the help of a kind parish priest, Fr. André, I decided on open adoption. I could pick the parents for my child and I would be able to visit him.

My water broke. It was time. Standing beside me in the labor room were Nell and Roger, the special couple I'd picked to be my baby's parents. Nell was trim, dark-haired, quiet. Roger, a lumberjack, had a bushy beard and a giant-sized heart.

The baby's head appeared. One more push. They laid little Ben on my abdomen. I loved him with all my heart . . . and so did Nell and Roger. Before he was cleaned up, Roger held him, bending over him face-to-face. "Don't cry little baby. Daddy's here."

We three shared him for three days. Once more, it was time. But unlike leaving Lisa with a social worker and walking away forever, this day rang with a future of hope. We assembled in my room: Roger, Nell, their two daughters, a friend from the music ministry at church, Fr. André, Ben, myself and even Mama.

Mama cried as she and my friend and I sang "Welcome to the Family" and "The Gift of Love." Fr. André conducted the ceremony. "Roger and Nell, do you take Ben to be your child, to rear him in love and in faith in God?"

"We do." •

I held Ben as Father André asked, "Heidi, do you in your love release Ben to his new parents?"

I looked at his tiny hands, his perfect little face, the sweet mouth. I knew that love had many forms. "I do." With simultaneous sorrow and joy I placed Ben in the arms of his parents. A kiss for Roger, for Nell and for our son.

After giving up Ben, I felt numb for a long time. When the numbness wore off, I felt broken. I wanted something but I didn't know what. I dated a couple of men, searching for affection and value. Instead, I began to feel used and devalued as a woman. I hated who I was. That only led to difficulties at work and more weight gain.

There was absolutely nothing in my life that was right. Then one night, desperate and alone, I reached back into the past. Past the men, past the adoptions, past the terrible Thing I couldn't mention, past the rejection of my family and friends, back, back into the prayers and retreats of my youth, to the times when I longed to come close to God. "O God, help me." It was a cry, a plea, a yearning.

* * *

Just when I needed it most, God brought three good people into my life. My job as a traveling nurse took me to Martha's Vineyard and I made friends with a couple and a priest. These three loving people actually treated me as if I was a valued person. They brought me into their spiritual walk and into their social lives. When I messed up, they didn't reject me. Instead they reinforced the lesson Eric had tried to get me to understand: that I really had value as a person.

Their love sent me to Medjugorje. On a mountain top, with the sun going down in the distance, the thought came to me that I needed to ask the Blessed Virgin Mary to direct my life.

Then I thought, no, that's silly.

But maybe she would.

Why would she help me?

Ask her.

Almost unwillingly, I took the step. "Mary, will you help me give my life completely to Jesus?"

How could I have ever guessed what would happen next?

One romance after another should have ended in bed, but it didn't. Some circumstance would prevent it. A guy's buddies would come and get him or a storm would come up out of nowhere or the communication between us would get messed up.

I spent a lot of lonely evenings trying to figure out what God was doing in my life. Now I understand that God was trying to wake up my conscience.

I moved to a small town and met Gene at a grocery store. This time the circumstances didn't prevent us from having sex. Two days later he called me, "I wrestled all night with God over what we did. Sex belongs to marriage, and I can't sleep with you unless we're married. It would be a sin. I don't ever want to wrestle like that with God again."

Sin? I'd caused him to sin? What did he mean? I was expressing my love fully and it didn't feel like sin to me. But my conscience woke up a little more. From then on, we cuddled and petted but we stayed out of bed.

I felt content just knowing that Gene wanted to marry me. Then, one weekend, he left for a fishing trip and I never saw him again.

During the days that followed, I found friendships in the music ministry at Mass and in a charismatic prayer group. Something quite remarkable happened next. I attended a seminar, and of all of the women God could have sent to be my prayer partner that day, the one he sent had a story especially for me . . . how she had changed from an adulterous woman to a woman of faith.

I told her truthfully, "I've only been chaste when a man had the strength to say no."

"What you've been doing is sin. And sin leads to death. Jesus wants you to live in his love and be forgiven."

Her words burned with truth. I started to think that I could be chaste.

But more than anything, it was good people who made the difference in my life. In the charismatic prayer meeting I was loved and accepted . . . and valued. I received much prayer for the little girl, Heidi, who had been betrayed.

Yet always in the background was the pain and loss of the abortion. It was the reason I'd drugged my conscience so completely. But I didn't know how to face it or what to do about it.

Then I met Sister Mary Frances. We were praying together at a retreat when she said, "I see an image of a knife." She waited for a moment. "Does that mean anything to you?"

Tears started falling. "I had an abortion." I told her my story, including going to confession and never feeling forgiven. She spoke lovingly of God's mercy.

As she prayed for me, I struggled to accept God's forgiveness and struggled to forgive myself. But there was so much guilt hidden away. So much sin. Pain that no one can describe. It was terrible to actually look at what I'd done. Sister prayed, "Dear Eternal Father, in your mercy look at Heidi with compassion and take away this pain that breaks her heart."

Somehow I understood that God had forgiven me for taking my child's life. After all the tears that I thought could ever fall, had fallen, Sister asked, "Have you named your child?"

"No."

We named her Alexis. I pictured Alexis in my mind, and together we placed her in Jesus' arms. Mary came into the picture and Alexis, now almost seven, stood between them. "I love you, Mommy, and I forgive you. And Jesus forgives you, too."

Cleansing tears soaked my blouse, "I love you, too, honey. I'm sorry."

After that, I went a long time without dating anyone and I was lonely. So I opened up my house to a friend just back from a month's vacation. Michael was someone I admired, a man who wanted to lead, and did lead, a chaste life. But while he had been on vacation he hadn't been able to attend Mass or do much praying.

An innocent hug turned into some heated kisses and snuggling before he called a halt to it. The next day, when we attended Mass he didn't receive Communion.

"Michael, why didn't you receive Communion?"

"I need to go to confession first."

"Why?"

"Because of what we did."

"Our actions kept you from receiving Jesus in the Eucharist?"

"Yes, I can't receive in a state of serious sin."

Serious sin? What did he mean? How much of my behavior had been more serious than I knew? I felt grief over causing Michael to feel apart from God. That meant I had affected our community, too. For the first time, I saw how my selfish longing to be held had wounded the Body of Christ. I went to confession, too.

Another realization. It was the Eucharist and confession and prayer that enabled Michael to be chaste. Separated from them, he was weak enough to give in to human desires. I began to pray more.

And I began to work on getting the past healed.

I forgave my father and brothers.

I asked God's forgiveness for all the promiscuity, for all the people I'd wounded by my life, for reading porno magazines and watching X-rated videos.

I prayed that Jesus would break every bond between me and each person I'd ever had sex with, and set me free to live a chaste life.

In prayer I cut all ties with unchastity between me and past generations of my family.

Then, joyfully, I journeyed to see Ben (the son placed in open adoption). I held him and read to him. His happy life gave me peace.

On the way home, I stopped at a Eucharistic Chapel for a visit. There God totally overwhelmed me by His loving Presence and personal love and care for me, a sinner. My heart could not hold all the love he poured into me.

I returned home full of joy and peace and willing to continue with the challenge to live a chaste life. Mass, Eucharist, Reconciliation, prayer, community, counseling. My conscience is alive. My healing journey goes on . . .

6

A Wild Irish Rose

Maureen O'Farrell

I had no idea that I was pretty. But as I look back at the pictures of myself, so tall and lithe, with my brown hair drawn back in French curls, I know now that I was. Just 17, I lived in my own apartment on a college campus in Idaho. Since school was my excuse to get away from home, everything about college life seemed super. Except for classes.

Because getting to class every day required more discipline than I had, I concentrated on the party life. That meant continuing the drug and alcohol abuse of my high school days. The party life in college also meant sex. Sex, I found out, was easy; just say Yes.

The first week in November I woke up with the flu, so ill I could hardly get to the bathroom. Later in the day I made my way to the campus infirmary. After a few questions the doctor asked, "Are you sexually active?"

"Yes, but what's that got to do with the flu?"

"I suspect your nausea is morning sickness. It's possible you're pregnant."

I felt like someone had jabbed me with a hypodermic needle full of numb. My brain refused to focus. I shook my head as if trying to get rid of her words.

After an exam she offered, "I'll make an appointment for an abortion."

"No, let me think."

"Consider it, it'll solve your problems."

Back at the apartment, I opened a can of beer so I could get hold of myself.

Oh, my God, what was my mother going to say? She was a single parent doing the best she could. She'd kill me. She was so strict about everything and so afraid I'd go to hell. I remember a time I stole a dime and then lied about it . . .

"Maureen, don't you ever, ever steal anything. You'll go to hell for stealing."

"Mama, it was only a dime."

She glared at me with that terrible stare, "What do you mean, only a dime? You lied about it, too. God will send you to hell for lying."

Those childhood conversations were still vivid, and now I was scared out of my mind what she would say when she found out I was pregnant.

I knew then that I couldn't tell her or anyone else. Not even my boyfriend. No one must know. What was it that the doctor had said about an abortion?

I walked into the clinic and paid my money at the counter like I was ordering a pair of jeans. I sat down as if I was waiting for someone to wrap them. If I was in a department store, then I couldn't be in an abortion clinic.

Four hours later I walked out of the clinic into a freezing winter afternoon. My whole body hurt. And something inside of me, not connected to my body, hurt even worse. *What had I done?* I shivered from head to foot. I'd just broken with every bit of moral background I'd been raised with. I'd paid $250.00 to commit murder.

In my apartment I climbed into bed and curled up in a ball. I was literally sick but at least no one knew what I'd done. By doing it alone, not telling anyone, I'd kept the perfect secret.

But as the day went on, a cold realization came to me. There was one person who knew. God. And I was going to hell for sure. I covered my head with the blankets and longed for the pain in my body and soul to go away.

When I woke up in the morning, the pain was still there. It was there the next day and the next. On Monday morning, I knew I had to go back to class but I just couldn't make myself do anything. I poured a drink and felt a whole lot better. I drank until I had the courage to get to class, except class was over.

I went home for Christmas with the decision already made that I would not, could not, go to Christmas Mass. But on Christmas Eve my godfather came to get me.

"No, I'm not going."

"Maureen, you will go."

I walked into that little church of my childhood and spent the most wretched hour of my life. All around me people were praying and singing, all part of a sacred circle, a circle that I could not get into. Everyone in this church would someday go to heaven. I would go to hell.

I wanted to make a run for the door. But I stayed: standing, sitting, kneeling. Full of sin. Every minute was a year. When would it be over? When could I escape? I knew that when I got out of there I'd never, never go into a Catholic church again.

Back at school in January it was more pain, alcohol, drugs, missed classes. By the end of the second semester, I moved back home with an incomplete in all my courses.

I knew I had to tell my Mom the awful secret that was eating me alive. Not only had I had sex out of wedlock, but I had murdered her grandchild.

"Mom."

"What is it, Maureen?"

"Nothing."

By the end of summer I made up my mind to tell her for sure.

In a way she opened up the conversation. Hesitantly she asked, "Maureen, you're sexually active, aren't you?"

"Yes."

She started the conversation and stopped. I could see the struggle this was for her. She wanted me to use birth control, but she didn't want to say it because it would sound like she was condoning sex outside of marriage.

Finally, I said, just to get it over with. "Mom, leave me alone. I'm sorry, but I've blown it and I know I'm going to hell anyway because I've already had an abortion."

I'll never forget the look on her face, like she'd been shot with a gun. I'd never seen such a look in anyone. There was no talk of hell or even of sex. She couldn't seem to say anything.

Up to that point I'd managed not to think about the abortion. But, touched by her shock, I could think of nothing else. By now the baby would have been born. I'd be holding it in my arms. If only I hadn't done what I'd done. Day after day I cried. But it was too late. I longed for another chance, another pregnancy, another child.

Then one morning I woke up with the solution. Why not get married?

Before I could find Mr. Right, I went to the hospital in excruciating pain. I had a severe pelvic inflammation and my liver was in bad shape from all the booze. A doctor, old and stern, warned, "Your tubes are so scarred, you've only a 50% chance of ever conceiving a child."

Dread washed over me. Had I killed the only child I would ever have? The guilt was so constant I felt like I was going crazy. As soon as I got out of the hospital I called a

Catholic church.   "I need to talk to a priest."

"This is Father Weston, can I help you?"

"I . . . I don't know. I've been in the hospital . . ." I couldn't say IT. Finally I stammered, "I need some guidance."

"My child, look to Jesus for your guidance.   Make a proclamation that Jesus Christ is the Lord of your life."

I hung up the phone and stared at the wall. Great! That's it? That's all I have to do? What on earth did he mean? I was 18. I was sick and needed help. God was mad at me. I was scared.

I didn't take the advice.

I knew what I needed. I needed a child. I needed to know if I could get pregnant. I figured out a plan for my own life. I'd quit drinking and doing drugs and I'd find someone stable to marry.

Nine months after I married Greg, I gave birth to a little girl I named Laura.   I couldn't take my eyes off of her. She was so beautiful. I held her to my breast and marveled at motherhood. I loved my little daughter deeply. Three years later I had another child, a boy I named Kevin.

But my marriage was failing. Greg and I didn't talk, didn't argue, didn't go anywhere, didn't do anything. It was so difficult being with him because I wanted friendship and conversation and fun. He wanted to watch television. Just when I needed most to get away, my uncle Bill said, "Come with me, I have a ranch in Montana."

Hoping for a new life, I took the children and left. But 400 marijuana plants greeted me at the ranch. I froze. No way. I'd said "No" to all this stuff, and if I got into it again I knew I couldn't be a good mother. Yet here was the temptation I couldn't resist. Desperately I called Greg, "Come over here. I need you."

What happened next is almost too horrible to tell. Greg and his best friend, Raul, came the next week, but instead of saving me from drugs, Greg just dumped himself into the drug scene. In retaliation I had a one-night affair with Raul.

So there I was, stuck in the life I'd figured out for myself. I had a four-year-old, a one-year-old, my husband was hooked on drugs and I was pregnant with his best friend's child.

To Raul the solution was easy, "Get an abortion."

"No, no, no!" I shrieked my refusal.

"There's no other way. I'm not supporting a kid."

"Yes, there is another way."

My new little son, whom I named Brian, was born beautiful and perfect. I counted each tiny pink toe. I memorized his sweet round face. In my love for him, I signed the papers for his adoption and wept my goodbye. A young couple gave my child a loving and stable home.

So much happened after that. Greg and I split up for good and Laura stayed with me. Even though I had legal custody of Kevin, he went to live with Greg. After I got Kevin back, I found out he'd been sexually abused.

Broken, defeated, useless. Twenty-six years old. I crawled into bed and wept. There was no hope for me. I was the worst person in the world. I had no friends. My mother had backed out of my life. I was doing drugs again. I'd conceived four children. One I'd killed, one I'd given away and one I'd allowed to live in a place where he'd been abused. Guilt overtook me. Failure seemed to suffocate me.

I hadn't prayed since I was 18. What was it that priest had said to do? Look to Jesus? I had absolutely nothing else left to do. "Jesus, my way is not working. I put myself in your hands. Send me an angel to get me out of this mess. Amen."

The next day I wondered, does God really hear the prayers of a person like me? I doubted it, but something did occur to me to do. It was almost like a message from God. Take the children to Sunday School.

There was a little neighborhood church close by. On Sunday I took Laura and Kevin by the hand, and the three of us went in together.

I settled the kids in their classes, and just as I was wondering what to do next, a man came up to me, "Hi, I'm John. The Lord has a message for you. He wants you to know that He is with you."

With me? I didn't know what to say but my knees felt weak.

He asked softly, "Is your life okay?"

I burst into tears. "No, no, nothing is right."

I felt a woman's arms go around me. "Honey, honey, honey, don't worry anymore. I'll be there for you." She was soft and motherly and her name was Jean.

Who were these people? All during the week that followed, I could hardly wait for next Sunday to see if I would meet them again.

The first person I saw was John. He hugged me and said a very strange thing. "The Lord told me he was giving me another daughter, and I would know her because her name would be familiar. Can you tell me your name?

"Maureen."

He burst into a huge smile. He'd just painted "Maureen" on the bow of his boat.

Jean joined us and he told her about my name. She was jubilant. Jean, who was married to John, opened her arms to me and I, with all my fears and loneliness, walked into them. I heard her say, "We know that God sent you to us. You are ours." Tears started rolling down my face.

Jean continued, "We know you have a chemical abuse problem, but whatever your needs are, for a home, for money, for help with the kids, think of us as your folks."

Almost out of nowhere, I had a family, parents to love and care about me and the children. I whispered, "Thank you, God." But as wonderful as Jean and John were to me, I abused their love. While they watched the kids, I went out drinking and doing drugs.

Still they loved me. Drawn by that love, I started reading the Bible. In a soft and quiet way I began to believe that God might love me, too. It was just a little belief and it wasn't there everyday, but sometimes I almost felt good. Other times I knew I was going to hell. Then I'd be back in a bar again.

Once more I got myself in trouble. Big trouble. I attacked a burglar and really hurt him. Then I met up with him in a bar. It was me against him and his six friends. I was a little drunk and a lot angry and ready to take them on all at once. Every eye was on me.

From across the room, a tough-looking motorcycle guy strode towards me. He had a full beard and thick black hair that stuck out a foot on each side of his head. He wore black leather and chains. He stopped inches away from me. "Don't fight these guys. You'll be hurt."

I was blazing mad and didn't want any interruptions. I *wanted* to fight this dude who'd burglarized me. I yelled at the stranger, "Get away from me, you old troll."

"I want to help you."

"I don't need your help."

I turned back to my fight but the guys had all backed away. I wasn't a threat to them but this new protector would scare anyone.

It turned out that the motorcycle guy's name was Ian, and although I accepted his offer of a ride home on his motorcycle, I wanted nothing to do with him. The next day he rang the doorbell. I warned Laura, "You tell him I'm not here."

I heard him say, "Here's something for your Mama." He handed her a red rose.

A rose? For me? For the worst person in the world? The next day he delivered another rose. The following day it was the same. Finally I agreed to have coffee with him.

Beneath the black leather and the wild hair was a man with the kindest heart I'd ever known. His eyes met mine, "Maureen, from the moment I saw you, the Lord said you were going to be my wife."

I laughed. "No way. Never."

But when I found out that he belonged to the motorcycle group that called themselves Hell's Angels, I didn't know whether to laugh or cry. I had asked God for an angel, but this wasn't what I'd meant. It was really strange. This guy couldn't be an answer to prayer. Could he?

Life definitely started getting better. I took Ian to meet John and Jean, and they welcomed him, two-foot beard, leather and chains, just as they'd welcomed me. He began attending the little neighborhood church, too. We were married, and Ian even prayed to God that I would have another child to take the place of the one who was adopted. I gave birth to a little girl I named Clare. I began to grow spiritually and learn how to pray to God. At last I said goodbye to drinking and drugs.

One day I came upon a car accident and saw a woman lying in the road. I jumped out of my car and ran to her. She had a six-inch gash in her head and blood was pouring down her face. "Oh, God, what should I do?"

I heard the answer so clearly that I looked around to see who'd spoken. "Pray."

I prayed with all my heart. To my astonishment the gash miraculously closed.

By now I was 33, Laura was thirteen, Kevin was nine, Clare was two. Ian and I and the children actually lived in a rose-covered cottage. Everything should have been great. But it wasn't.

I was haunted by the abortion. When things were bad, I hadn't worried about the abortion because I felt like I was constantly being punished for it. But now life was good to me. And I didn't deserve goodness.

If only I hadn't done it. If only I could bring my child back. If only I hadn't walked into that clinic that day more than 14 years ago. I wept before God: I'm so sorry, so sorry, so sorry. Being sorry didn't help.

The abortion was under the surface of every minute, eating away my life. Physically I felt dizzy at the oddest times. Some days I didn't even have the strength to do my work. Sometimes I absolutely had to have quiet because there was so much blame going on in my head that I couldn't think if there was any noise. Across my shoulders hung a steel chain of guilt and shame.

In the little church they said that God forgave every sin, but I couldn't feel forgiven. I suffered every day knowing that despite my prayers, God could never forgive someone like me.

Then the accident happened.

I'll never forget how the day that changed my life began . . .

It was 8:00 in the morning, Laura had just left to catch the school bus that stopped across the road and Kevin started out the door behind her, "Bye, Mom."

"Come back and give me a kiss."

He zipped back in, popped a kiss on my cheek and raced across the road.

I heard a screech. And then a thud. So loud the sound filled the house. I raced to the road, knowing before I reached it what I would find.

Kevin's body lay sprawled on the pavement. "My baby, my baby." I put my hands under his head. His whole body was limp, his eyes were open and vacant.

A green truck was stopped in the middle of the road, a four-inch dent in its hood. I knew that Kevin's head, the lifeless little head beneath my hands, had made that dent. The police came. One of them wrote, "Dead on the scene."

I cried out to God. "No, no, not my baby. Give me my child, return him to me. Don't let him die and don't let him live and be a vegetable. Oh God, oh God, return him and make him whole. Please God, oh God, oh God." I visualized his brain and liver and lungs and kidneys and heart all whole and functioning. "Make him whole and spotless. Please God."

The policeman wanted me to move.

"Oh God, my son. Restore him to a normal nine-year-old."

"You're hysterical, lady, stop this. He's been dead 10 minutes."

"Please, please, please, God, bring him back."

"I'm going to have to slap you if you don't stop."

Our neighbor, T.J., spoke sharply to the policeman, "Haven't you ever heard anyone pray?"

"Is that praying?"

"Oh God, I place him wholly in your will. If you take him, that's all right, but if you leave him, restore him."

T.J. put his hand on Kevin's pulse and shouted, "We got him back!" "We got him back!"

I wondered, why is he shouting?

T.J. yelled, "He's alive! Kevin's alive!"

The policeman stared at T.J. and then at Kevin. Clearly he couldn't believe his eyes.

The crowd with tears running down their faces, whispered to one another, "He's alive!" Everyone pressed in closer.

So much confusion followed. A hearse had been ordered. Now an ambulance was needed instead.

It was a miracle. God had given a miracle to Kevin . . . and to me.

All of a sudden Kevin's body flipped up from the pavement and a scream louder than any scream I've ever heard came out of his mouth. My son was alive.

In the hospital I sat beside Kevin and held his small hand. I had so many questions about what had happened. But the strangest question of all I asked myself: "Maureen, how are you different?" For I knew that deep inside me, something had changed.

Understanding came. The steel chain of guilt and shame that had laid across my shoulders was gone. I was different. I was free.

How did it happen? How could it happen? The answer was crystal clear. If God can raise the dead, he can forgive every sin.

Two months passed, glorious months. Kevin returned home completely normal. I saw the whole world differently. I knew without a shadow of a doubt that when God forgives He forgives totally, even the killing of a baby.

Kevin was different, too. He was more serious. One afternoon, as we were riding in the car, he said, "God spoke to me. He said, 'Enter into my tent and my tent only.'"

At first I didn't pay much attention to him because it sounded so strange and so unlike anything Kevin would say.

He said it again. "Mama, God said, 'Enter into my tent and my tent only.'"

Ian and I both looked at him, "What does that mean? Where is God's tent? If you tell us where it is, we'll go with you."

"That little brown building by the super-market, that's God's tent."

In a surprised voice Ian said, "That's the Catholic church."

I felt my eyes fill with tears. I could never go there. I remembered that Mass I'd been to when I was 18. I'd known I was going to hell. Every time I ever thought of Mass I thought of hell. Tears were running down my face as I told Ian and Kevin, "I can't go into a Catholic church. I'm too scared."

Ian looked at me with such surprise and his words were a reproach, "I thought you said you were forgiven."

"You don't understand." I was shaking all over. "I'm not afraid of God, I'm afraid of the Catholic Church."

Ian said quietly, "I'll take Kevin if you don't want to go."

They went together and that was fine. To me a Catholic church was the scariest place on earth.

Meanwhile, my friend Barbara begged me, "Maureen, come to Mass with me. There's a priest you have to meet."

"No."

"Please, his name is Father Guillermo. He's a wonderful priest."

"Never." The thought made my whole insides churn.

"Not for your sake but for mine."

I groaned. Barbara was so good to me. At last I agreed. "Only for your sake. Not for mine."

At Mass I knelt beside Barbara and watched this priest who was supposed to be so special. He was old, gray, but . . . but he was so serene. At the Consecration, I watched carefully. "This is My Body."

I shivered. Old memories and then doubts flooded me, Deliberately I questioned, "Lord, is that really you?"

At Communion time, I felt a nudge. Barbara wanted me to move over. I moved. Another nudge. I moved again. One more nudge and I was pushed right off the pew. Startled, I stood up. There was Fr. Guillermo in front of me giving out Communion. "Body of Christ." On instinct I put out my tongue. Then he did something I've never seen before or since. He took my hand and led me to the Cup. "The Blood of Christ." I drank from the Cup. I was so touched by God I felt like I might fall over.

Father looked me in the eye, "Was there ever any doubt?"

I went back to the pew with my mind reeling. There was Barbara kneeling at the other end. If she was still there, then who had nudged me?

I was still in a fog at the coffee hour when Barbara asked, "Did you see the angel?"

"What angel?"

"There was one beside you at Mass. I thought that was why you moved."

So God had sent a real angel after all. When I'd prayed for an angel, I could never have guessed the many ways He would answer.

All of a sudden I had to talk to Fr. Guillermo. I almost dragged him to the corner. "Please, I have something to say. I went to Communion without going to confession."

His blue eyes, overflowing with goodness, looked into mine. "I know. That's why I gave you absolution before you received." He smiled, "I'll see you next Saturday for confession at 3:00."

On Saturday I told myself that I didn't need to go. But I got in the car anyway. I argued, I don't need this. But I kept driving. As I turned a corner, the sun shone in the western sky as a ball of red. Red like the blood of Jesus. Round like the Host. I drove to the church without anymore argument.

I confessed it all. Even the abortion. Whatever would my penance be? Out of the kindness of this priest's holy heart, he knew I needed something hard but doable. "Take Holy Communion at Mass every Sunday for a year."

"How can I? My marriage . . ."

"God wants you in the Church. Your marriage will be straightened out."

That was Christmas time. In the fall, our marriage was blessed. By the next summer, Ian and the children and my dear parents, Jean and Joe, were all baptized. Today I know with deep joy and clarity what it means to be totally forgiven by Jesus and restored. Laura, Kevin, Clare and the new baby Kathleen, Ian and me, all of us are touched by the goodness of God.

Editor's note: At a parish dinner I attended with Maureen and her family, someone began to complain about their noisy, burglarizing, motorcycling neighbors. "Tell them God loves them," Maureen said. The other conversations stopped and all eyes were on her. She continued, "I know. I rode a motorcycle. I did terrible things. I broke God's rules but God never stopped loving me. You go tell those guys that God's never going to stop loving them, no matter what they do."

Psycho-Spiritual Healing AFTER Abortion
by Douglas R. Crawford and Michael T. Mannion

A helpful book for those who seek to counsel a woman who has had an abortion: for the psychologist who recognizes the importance of faith in the struggle to be whole, and for the clergyperson who recognizes that it is inadequate to expect that "God will do it all."

LL1246, 104 pp, pb, **$6.95**

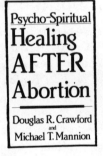

Post-Abortion Aftermath: A ComprehensiveConsideration
edited by Michael T. Mannion

Essays presented at the Post-Abortion Summit Conference, Washington, DC, September 1993. Studies are just beginning to reveal the devastating, long-term spiritual and emotional effects suffered by women who choose to have abortions.

LL1707, 190 pp, pb, **$12.95**